Contents

MAIN COVER IMAGE: XS235 in flight. (Gordon Bain)

INSET COVER: A 51 Squadron Comet 2R at Sharjah in 1962. (Peter Aitkens)

INSET COVER: A BEA Airtours Comet 4B taxies at Gatwick. (Chris England)

THIS PAGE: XS235 *Canopus* was the final flying Comet, retiring in 1997. (Gordon Bain)

ISBN 9781802822151
Editor: Jon Lake and Angie Bee
Senior editor, specials: Roger Mortimer
Email: roger.mortimer@keypublishing.com
Design: SJmagic DESIGN SERVICES, India.
Cover: Dan Jarman

Advertising Sales Manager: Brodie Baxter
Email: brodie.baxter@keypublishing.com
Tel: 01780 755131

Advertising Production: Debi McGowan
Email: debi.mcgowan@keypublishing.com

SUBSCRIPTION/MAIL ORDER
Key Publishing Ltd, PO Box 300, Stamford, Lincs, PE9 1NA
Tel: 01780 480404 Fax: 01780 757812
Subscriptions email: subs@keypublishing.com
Mail Order email: orders@keypublishing.com
Website: www.keypublishing.com/shop

PUBLISHING
Group CEO: Adrian Cox
Publisher: Jonathan Jackson
Head of Publishing: Finbarr O'Reilly
Head of Marketing: Shaun Binnington

Key Publishing Ltd, PO Box 100, Stamford, Lincs, PE9 1XP
Tel: 01780 755131
Website: www.keypublishing.com

PRINTING
Precision Colour Printing Ltd, Haldane, Halesfield 1, Telford, Shropshire. TF7 4QQ

DISTRIBUTION
Seymour Distribution Ltd, 2 Poultry Avenue, London, EC1A 9PU
Enquiries Line: 02074 294000.

The de Havilland Comet – The World's First Jetliner

Co-author Jon Lake sums up what the de Havilland Comet – the first airliner of its type – represented in the development of civil and later military aviation.

BELOW: **The aircraft that flew the world's first jet airliner service was BOAC's G-ALYP. Less than two years later, the aircraft was lost in the first of two fatal accidents that led to the type's grounding.**

It is 70 years since the de Havilland Comet entered commercial service. Still one of the prettiest and most graceful-looking airliners to take to the air, it is hard to appreciate today just how astonishingly futuristic the aircraft seemed in 1949. When the prototype made its Farnborough debut that year it was as fast as the new jet fighters and jet bombers that displayed alongside it.

And on May 2, 1952, when G-ALYP call sign 'Yoke Peter' inaugurated a scheduled jet service between London and Johannesburg, the Comet appeared to have catapulted Britain into a leading position in the air transport industry. This was, after all, the world's first jetliner flight with fare-paying passengers on board. The Comet set new standards in speed, smoothness, and a quiet cabin environment. Mike Ramsden, the editor of *Flight*, and a former de Havilland apprentice, called it "the biggest step forward ever taken in airliner design."

And the Comet made the world sit up and take notice, challenging as it did comfortable notions that jet propulsion was in some way 'excessive' for civil aviation. In Seattle and Long Beach, US rivals certainly took notice, and began working on their own jetliners, but Boeing and Douglas faced a mountain to climb if they were to catch up with de Havilland.

But despite being a ground-breaking technological achievement, despite becoming the world's first commercial

jet airliner, and despite ushering in a new era of commercial air travel the Comet has left behind it something of a 'mixed' reputation.

The glory won by the Comet was tarnished early on by a series of fatal accidents. Even after the causes of these were discovered, and even after a major redesign, public confidence in the aircraft never fully returned, and sales were badly affected.

After three Comets broke up in flight, the Comet's Certificate of Airworthiness was revoked in 1954, the Comet 1 was grounded, and the Comet 2 never entered full airline service.

But a handful of modified Comet 1s (and the new Comet 2s) did continue flying as military transports, and testing of the Comet 3 continued while de Havilland forged ahead with the development of its definitive 'intercontinental' Comet 4.

De Havilland's faith and confidence in the Comet's fundamentally sound design was validated on October 4, 1958 when BOAC inaugurated the first scheduled transatlantic jet services with its new Comet 4s, scoring another first. This has often been interpreted as having been something of a pyrrhic victory, on the basis that Boeing's new 707 soon began doing the same thing between New York and Paris – starting Transatlantic services on October 26.

And while the Boeing 707 undoubtedly took sales away from the Comet, with its higher capacity and faster speed, the British jetliner enjoyed real success, and the aircraft fitted some niches better than its American rival, not least thanks to its superior take off performance, which allowed it to operate from shorter runways. But the Comet could also turn a profit with lower passenger numbers, allowing it to operate profitably on thinner routes, and on developing routes.

De Havilland originally projected a 'break-even' point for the Comet 4 family of 67 sales. In the end, though, the break-even figure for the Comet Mk.4 was the sale of just 57 aircraft. By the time production ceased more than 70 Mk.4s (and Mk 4 sub-variants) had been sold, making the Comet a success, even in strictly commercial terms. De Havilland was able to pay back a £4m loan from the British Government, and to generate a £1.5m profit for the British taxpayer!

And you'd have to be uncharitable not to acknowledge that the Boeing 707 and the later Douglas DC-8 owed much of their success to the Comet, since both incorporated lessons from the Comet 1 disasters into their designs.

Above all the Comet was first. It was the Comet that pointed the way to the future for the airline transport industry, and that showed how jet airliners could open up the world and democratise air travel. Comets also gave sterling service as testbeds and a handful of SIGINT-configured Comets were among the most important reconnaissance aircraft of the Cold War.

While aircraft like the Comet and the Viscount may not have provided the basis for a truly self-sustaining, export-rich, highly-profitable civil aerospace sector, they were impressive technological achievements, and did enjoy success. They kept jobs and government spending in the UK and helped to reduce the balance of payments. And while government support for civil aircraft programmes between 1945 and 1951 amounted to £40.65m, levies on sales over the same period returned £12.35m to the Exchequer, and continued sales of some types throughout the 1950s returned even more money to the public coffers.

And though the Comet did experience a number of fatal crashes that shattered its reputation and eroded its market lead, the aircraft is one that deserves to be celebrated and remembered with a degree of pride.

The Comet's first pilot, John Cunningham, once described the aircraft as "one of the most significant aeroplanes in the entire history of commercial air transport."

It's hard to disagree with his assessment, and that's why we believe that the Comet richly deserves this anniversary tribute. We hope that you enjoy reading it as much as we enjoyed putting it together!

But putting together a volume like this is very much a team effort, and we'd like to thank Key Publishing for commissioning, supporting, and guiding us, the irrepressible Rolando Ugolini for his breathtakingly colourful artwork, Comet historians Philip Birtles and Martin Painter for their inspiration and generosity, and our friends, old and new, for helping out with photos. So many thanks go to Peter Aitkens, Alan Allen, Urs Baettig, Terry Campbell, Caz Caswell, Dave Donald, Chris England, Reto Fasciatti, Rob Feeley, Martin Fisher, Graeme Gibson, Lewis Grant, Rob Hodgkins, Ian Joslin, Manfred Kaffine, Norbert Krîpfl, Chris Martin, Malcolm Nason, Alan Pratt, Stefan Röhrich, Nick Stone, Alan Wilson, Gordon Bain, Graham Dives, Ken Fielding, Ian Haskell and David Whitworth.

Finally, we'd like to dedicate this to all those who flew the Comet – and particularly those who flew it with 192 and 51 Squadrons. Special mention goes to the late Group Captain Derek Rake, and to Air Commodore Danny Honley, Mr Eric Quinney, Wing Commander Ron Haddow, Ron Boreham, and Alan Dawes, whose story we hope to bring you in a future volume.

Jon Lake and Angie Bee

ABOVE: It is now 70 years since the de Havilland Comet flew the world's first jetliner service, on May 2, 1952. BOAC made sure that even the bus to the aircraft was suitably decorated!

LEFT: Four years after BOAC's Comet fleet was grounded, the new Comet 4 set new records, and demonstrated that de Havilland's Comet was back! G-APDA was the first of 19 Comet 4s built for BOAC.

The Birth of the de Havilland Comet

With its name derived from a racing type and its original development begun in the dark days of World War Two, the Comet was about to rewrite the rule book for civil aviation.

RIGHT: The Comet's name was borrowed from the company's DH88 racer, which had won the 1934 MacRobertson London to Melbourne Air Race.

BELOW: The Comet prototype in flight, showing off the type's elegant lines, and its modestly swept wing. The aircraft initially flew under a 'B-class' registration, G-5-1, before being re-registered as G-ALVG on September 1, 1949.

On December 23, 1942, with the outcome of the war far from being a foregone conclusion, the British government set up a new committee within the Ministry of Aircraft Production. This was tasked with considering the post-war civil aviation requirements of Britain and the Commonwealth. Lord Brabazon of Tara (holder of the first British pilot's licence) was appointed to chair the committee, which went on to produce two reports which together outlined a programme of post-war civil airliner development, and which described a list of nine suggested aircraft 'Types' – five of them new developments. Though the eponymous Bristol Brabazon (which represented 'Type I') was a failure, the Brabazon Committee report also launched the development of the de Havilland Dove (Type V), the Airspeed Ambassador and Vickers Viscount (Type II), the Bristol Britannia (Type III) and the de Havilland Comet (Type IV).

The Type IV was originally seen as a fast, jet-powered, transatlantic mail plane that could also perhaps carry a small number of VIP passengers, but at the urging of one of the committee members, Geoffrey de Havilland, the aircraft grew in size to become a 100-seat, high-speed jet airliner.

De Havilland had an impressive pedigree when it came to the design and development of very high-speed aircraft. During World War One, the DH4 had been faster than any contemporary fighter, while in World War Two, the de Havilland Mosquito enjoyed a similar reputation. And

by 1943 de Havilland's design team, including the then 72-year-old design engineer CC Walker, believed that this kind of high speed would even be possible in a civil airliner.

De Havilland enjoyed a real advantage in that the de Havilland Engine Company, under the leadership of Major Frank Halford, was already establishing a real lead in jet engine technology. The Halford H1, later known as the de Havilland Goblin engine was so advanced that it was actually used to power the Gloster Meteor prototype on its maiden flight on March 5, 1943, because the selected Rolls Royce Welland (developed from the original, better known Whittle turbojet) was not ready in time. While sticking with a conservative centrifugal flow compressor, the developed de Havilland Ghost engine was even more impressive. Originally developed for the new Venom fighter bomber, the Ghost was developed from the earlier Goblin that powered the Vampire and proved more powerful, more reliable, and with better fuel consumption. The Ghost received its type approval on June 28, 1948 and is today remembered as the first practical commercial jet engine. Crucially, the engine's reliability, and the speed, altitude, and smoothness it conferred on the Comet confounded conventional opinion that the high fuel consumption of the jet engine would prevent any jet airliner from being a commercial success.

One early de Havilland jet airliner design used a scaled-up Vampire type configuration with three Goblin (later three Ghost) engines in the rear of the fuselage pod, carrying 20 passengers over a 700 mile range. Another early study used three engines buried in the rear fuselage, with a rear-mounted straight wing and canard foreplanes. But straight-winged jet designs would soon give way to something more radical.

After the war, de Havilland engineers were among the experts dispatched to occupied Germany to assess German progress in aeronautics. Ronald Bishop, de Havilland's chief designer, and Richard Clarkson, the chief aerodynamicist, returned from Germany convinced of the need to use a swept wing, and a tailless airliner design, with a 40° swept wing and four Ghost engines, was rapidly drawn up. A Vampire airframe was used as the basis for the DH108 which was used to explore the configuration, and the DH108 Swallow subsequently became the first British aircraft to break the sound barrier.

By May 1946, the proposed airliner was expected to weigh in at 82,000lb, and had gained a horizontal tail, which promised to allow higher take-off and landing weights when using the same runway length.

The Ministry of Supply ordered two prototypes in September 1946, and detailed design, to meet a BOAC specification, began on September 27, 1946. BOAC agreed

to a halving of leading edge sweep to 20° to increase the maximum lift coefficient and reduce the structural weight, as well as a lengthening of the fuselage to increase passenger capacity, and the substitution of unswept tail surfaces for the swept tailplanes and fin. Some consideration was given to using one of the new axial flow turbojets then under development, but a perceived susceptibility to FOD (Foreign Object Damage) prevented this, and the robust simplicity of the centrifugal Ghost won the day.

On that same evening, September 27, 1946, chief test pilot Geoffrey de Havilland was killed while flying the DH108. This led his father, company chairman Sir Geoffrey de Havilland to appoint John Cunningham as the new chief test pilot. To prepare himself for flying the new de Havilland DH106 airliner, Cunningham gained some airliner experience on BOAC's Lockheed 049 Constellations, including transatlantic flights and one long flight to Sydney. He thereby gained invaluable experience of airline practices and operating procedures.

A complete weight and performance statement for what was now the DH106 was prepared in November 1946, describing an aircraft capable of carrying a 7,000lb payload (or 24 passengers) from London to Gander with fuel for diversions, and allowing for a 100mph headwind. On Empire routes the aircraft would carry 32 passengers over stages of up to 2,200 miles.

Unlike aircraft such as the Avro Ashton and the Avro Canada C-102 Jetliner, the de Havilland DH106 was more than just a jet-powered counterpart to contemporary propeller driven airliners. Nor were the Comet's modestly swept wings the key to the aircraft's success, and they did not justify its claim to be a genuinely revolutionary development.

ABOVE: The de Havilland DH108 Swallow assessed one of the configurations considered for the DH106. The tailless aircraft had 40° of wing sweep, and all three prototypes were lost in accidents. The third prototype, VW120, is seen here with the world altitude record-breaking Vampire, TG278.

BELOW: The Comet prototype seen being prepared for an early test flight. The two prototypes were fitted with single wheel main undercarriage units, unlike production Comets, which used four-wheeled bogies.

The DH106 was the first production airliner whose wing formed an integral fuel tank, the first to use pressure refuelling, and the first with hydraulically operated, power-boosted controls with simulated (artificial) feel and no manual backup. These were thoroughly evaluated in ground rigs, and on one of the three DH108s. The new airliner was also, in its production form, the first to have a multi wheel landing gear!

The anticipated operating altitude of the DH106 meant that it would require pressure differentials nearly twice as high as those on existing airliners, and it was recognised that a cabin pressurisation failure could be catastrophic. Accordingly, the cabin was designed never to fail, and was rigorously tested in water tanks, until everyone was confident that the new jetliner could withstand decades of operation at high altitude.

To manufacture the DH106, de Havilland invested £1m in new tooling, including drop hammers, stretch presses and Hufford tools, and advanced jigs that allowed more of the production process to be undertaken by semi-skilled workers.

The Ministry of Supply issued an instruction to proceed with eight aircraft on January 21, 1947, at BOAC's request, and at a fixed price of £250,000 per aircraft, including £45,000 for the four Ghost turbojets. The BOAC order was eventually fixed at nine aircraft, following its merger with BSAA, which had ordered six DH106s.

Before the prototypes could fly, the new Ghost engines were evaluated in the outboard nacelles of an Avro Lancastrian, VM703, which took to the air in its new guise on July 24, 1947, soon being joined by another, VM749. On March 23, 1948, Cunningham flew a Ghost-engined Vampire (TG278), converted as a high altitude testbed for the engine, to set a record-breaking height of 59,446 feet.

Doubts as to the view from the DH106 windscreen led to the construction of a mock up nose that was fitted to an

Airspeed Hotspur II glider (TL348) which was then flown by Cunningham in March and April 1947, towed aloft behind a Handley Page Halifax 'tug'.

The new DH106 was named Comet in December 1947, reviving the name previously used by the de Havilland DH88 racing aircraft. The original Comet had been developed specifically to participate in the 1934 MacRobertson Air Race from England to Australia, which it won, beating the Douglas DC-2 and Boeing 247 high-speed airliners.

The actual Comet prototype was rolled out for engine runs on April 2, 1949 (engines then only being fitted to port), and then, with all four engines fitted, for taxiing trials on July 25, 1949.

On July 27, the shared birthday of both Cunningham and Sir Geoffrey de Havilland, the Comet underwent further taxi and brake tests, followed by three short hops to test elevator, aileron, and rudder responsiveness. The press had been invited to witness the high speed runs and departed that afternoon.

The absence of 'snags' led to Cunningham's decision, late in the day, to make the aircraft's maiden flight, accompanied by co-pilot John Wilson, and flight test observer Tony Fairbrother, with Frank Reynolds as flight engineer hydraulics and Tubby Waters as flight engineer electrics.

Many in the press assumed that de Havilland had attempted to exclude them from the first flight, and some were angry about it. The aviation correspondent for *The Times* was so cross that he swore that he'd never mention de Havilland again!

Early flight trials proved the Comet's pleasant and viceless handling characteristics, with a stall described as 'gentlemanly' and 'like a big Vampire'. The aircraft even managed to achieve Mach 0.8 in a shallow dive on August 8, 1949. Jet fighters frequently tried to 'pop up'

BELOW: The highly-polished second prototype, G-ALZK, is seen being prepared for her maiden flight on 27 July 1950. The aircraft was soon loaned to BOAC for route-proving flights.

LEFT: The Comet second prototype, G-ALZK, is seen here at Johannesburg's Palmietfontein Airport, wearing full BOAC livery, in June 1951. One year later, Palmietfontein was the destination for the first BOAC Comet service.

for a look, but few were able to intercept the Comet or keep up with it.

Cunningham took the Comet prototype (by now registered G-ALVG) to London Airport on October 22 and 23, flying a series of GCA approaches and night landings and demonstrating the aircraft's ability to 'slot into' the pattern alongside piston-engined airliners. At 0533 on the second day, the Comet took off and headed for Castel Benito airport outside Tripoli, arriving three hours and 23 minutes later. The return flight was made in three hours and 15 minutes.

This and other long distance flights confirmed de Havilland's performance predictions – the Comet proved able to cruise at 490mph at heights of up to 40,000ft,

carrying 36 passengers. With ground running, taxiing, take-off, and the climb, plus the descent, circuit, approach, and landing, it was calculated that the Comet had a still air range of 2,645 miles.

The first prototype was used for an initial air-to-air refuelling trial, and for testing of Napier Sprite rocket motors. These burned for 12 seconds on take-off, and gave 5,000lb of extra thrust – briefly the equivalent of two extra Ghost engines! In the end, neither air-to-air refuelling nor rocket assisted take-off gear was adopted for airline service, both being considered unnecessary.

A second prototype, G-ALZK, made its maiden flight on July 27, 1950, and joined the flight test programme before being loaned to BOAC for training and route-proving.

BELOW: The second prototype was a well-travelled aircraft, flying to Rome, Nicosia, and Cairo in May 1951, and then to Khartoum, Entebbe, and Livingstone in June. Subsequent destinations included Baghdad, Basrah, Karachi, Bombay, Puna, Kallang, and Bangkok.

de Havilland DH.106 Comet 1 prototype
Prototype G-5-1, Ministry of Supply/de Havilland

c/n 06001, **Fate:** Scrapped at Farnborough, late 1950s

Ordered by the Ministry of Supply under Specification 20/44 (as one of a pair of prototypes, the other being G-ALZK), the Comet prototype was rolled out in April 1949, and undertook engine runs before making a maiden flight on July 27, 1949, in the hands of de Havilland chief test pilot John 'Cat's Eyes' Cunningham. This unusual nickname originated during World War Two, when Cunningham had served as a distinguished night fighter pilot. Not wanting to draw attention to the use and effectiveness of airborne radar, the Air Ministry created a cover story to explain Cunningham's successes as the first night fighter ace. It was said that Cunningham's eyesight was so exceptional that it allowed him to see in the dark with the same visual acuity as a domestic cat - thanks in part to his carrot-rich diet which supposedly provided him with sufficient vitamin A to maintain excellent night-vision! The prototype Comet was initially finished in highly polished aluminium overall.

The Comet prototype made a series of short 'hops' from Hatfield's runway on July 27 to allow Cunningham to check the operation of the flight controls, with senior managers and government officials watching, and with the press gathered to 'preview' the first flight, which was then scheduled for later in the week. After the press and VIP guests had departed, however, Cunningham decided to make the maiden flight that evening!

He took off at 18:17 and landed 31 minutes later, having taken the aircraft to a height of 8,000 ft. The flight ended with a low flypast for those workers still on site!

"She's very promising so far," Cunningham commented after landing.

ABOVE: **The first prototype initially flew with leading edge slats outboard, though these were locked shut after the fourth flight, when stalling tests showed they were not necessary. Fences were added, however.**

The prototype was first flown with a 'B-class' registration (G-5-1), and with leading edge slats fitted, but the slats were locked shut after the fourth flight and the aircraft was re-registered as G-ALVG on 1 September, in preparation for its 1949 Farnborough Airshow appearance. The Comet prototype was fitted with a nose-mounted instrumentation boom.

BELOW: **The first prototype is seen here during an early test flight, wearing the registration G-5-1 on the rear fuselage and a de Havilland logo high on the tailfin.**

de Havilland DH.106 Comet 1 prototype
Prototype, G-ALVG, Ministry of Supply/de Havilland

c/n 06001, **Fate:** Scrapped at Farnborough, late 1950s

In its initial guise, the Comet prototype was finished in highly polished aluminium overall. Other markings were at first limited to a small de Havilland logo on the fin top, and 'DE HAVILLAND COMET' on the forward fuselage. In these colours, G-ALVG stole the show at the 1949 Farnborough Airshow, and was soon 'back at work', with Cunningham flying circuits and working the pattern at London Airport a few days later, prior to an overseas trip to Tripoli on October 25, 1949. A second overseas trip was made to Rome in March 1950, followed by tropical trials at Cairo in Egypt and Nairobi in Kenya in April 1950.

By September 1950, a BOAC Speedbird had been applied to the nose, later joined by a Union flag on the tail fin. Finally, the aircraft was painted in full BOAC colours, with a white fuselage top and a blue cheatline.

After basic testing and envelope expansion, G-ALVG was used for testing the new four-wheeled main undercarriage bogies (these had to be locked down, as the main gear wheel wells could not accommodate the new design), and, after the original undercarriage was refitted, for hot and high trials at Khartoum and Nairobi. The aircraft was used for trial fitting and testing of Napier Sprite rocket assisted take-off gear and assessed the new 'drooped' wing leading edge - fitted to solve a stall issue.

The prototype was used for a number of overseas flights and was displayed at the 1951 SBAC air show at Farnborough. Less than two years later, on July 31, 1953, G-ALVG made her final flight to Farnborough for structural testing, focused mainly on

ABOVE: **The first Comet prototype soon gained a BOAC 'Speedbird' logo on her nose, and a Union Flag on her tailfin. Here she is seen taxiing out in front of a crowd of smartly attired journalists. Overcoats and hats are no longer in vogue for journalists, alas!**

wing loading. The aircraft was placed in open storage in 1955, with major assemblies cocooned, and was then scrapped during the late 1950s.

With their single-wheel main undercarriage units and just eight windows on each side of the fuselage, the Comet prototypes differed in detail from the subsequent Comet 1 production variant.

BELOW: **Both prototypes ended their flying careers wearing full BOAC markings. Only the single mainwheels distinguish G-ALVG from a production Comet 1, externally, at least.**

The World's First Jetliner

To a generation of hardy air travellers used to the deafening noise of the big propliners, jolting along in the worst of the weather, the Comet seemed like something out of Dan Dare – fast, quiet and above all smooth.

RIGHT: BOAC pilots soon took to the Comet, which proved to have a compelling blend of delightful handling characteristics and superb performance. After aircraft like the Argonaut, the Hermes, the Stratocruiser, and the Constellation, it felt like the future!

BELOW: The first production Comet 1, G-ALYP, leads the two prototypes during an early flight from Hatfield. The aircraft made its maiden flight on January 9, 1951 and was delivered to BOAC on March 13.

Despite the appearance of the Comet prototypes at Farnborough Airshows and on route-proving flights, its introduction on scheduled services with fare-paying passengers on May 2, 1952, was a truly seismic event. Its impact was comparable to, or perhaps even greater than, the launch of supersonic services by Concorde 24 years later.

In both cases 'ordinary' men and women were suddenly able to fly at speeds and heights that had hitherto been the exclusive domain of small numbers of elite military pilots. They needed no special training and no exceptional levels of fitness. And they could do so in shirtsleeves, with their ordinary hats and coats stowed on luggage racks or in cloakrooms, being served food and drinks by smart stewards and pretty stewardesses. They did not have to be trussed up in g-suits and did not have to wear uncomfortable bone domes and oxygen masks.

Both aircraft incorporated astonishing new technologies and innovation, and both cost much more than the

previous generation of airliners and burned twice as much fuel (though the Comet was burning Kerosene, which was significantly cheaper than the high octane Avgas used by the big propliners). And both aircraft types slashed journey times, and both seemed to be the standard bearers of a new age in air travel.

But while Concorde remained something of a 'flash in the pan' – being built in tiny numbers and failing to kick-start a new generation of supersonic airliners, the Comet saw widespread service in its own right, and also ushered in the age of the jet airliner.

And the Comet brought with it an entirely new experience of air travel. The previous generation of propliners were noisy, and dragged their passengers through the weather, where they were buffeted by wind and turbulence in cabins that were often a cacophony of vibration and unpleasant smells! The Comet cruised serenely above the weather, allowing a young passenger to build a 'house of cards' on his table if he or she chose! The cabin environment provided a completely new experience. By contrast, a Concorde passenger just got to his destination rather more quickly than he would have done on a VC10 or Boeing 707.

PROFITABLE

And from the start, the Comet made real profits for its operators – not just providing a 'halo effect' but earning revenues that outweighed costs. The Comets made sufficient profit in their first year of operation to cover interest on capital, and it was expected that the cost of training and route-proving would be spread over the planned life of the aircraft.

The Comet even proved less maintenance intensive than the propliners that went before, with an engine change taking 12 man hours compared to 40 on a Stratocruiser.

BOAC also found the Comet to be more productive than its predecessors, calculating that five Comets could do the work of eight older airliners.

And this productivity and profitability were apparent from the start, with the initial production Comet 1 variant. The first production Comet 1, registered G-ALYP, made its maiden flight on January 9, 1951 and was subsequently lent to BOAC for development flying by its Comet Unit at London Airport and at Hurn, initially operating alongside the second prototype, G-ALZK.

The unit was headed by BOAC captain MJR 'Roly' Alderson, and included Captains Ernie Rodley, Cliff Alabaster, and Alastair Majendie, with John Cunningham and Peter Buggé from de Havilland also sharing the flying. Alderson was a long-serving BOAC pilot who had flown the Empire Class flying boat, Rodley and Alabaster were former Pathfinders, who had flown the Lancaster and Mosquito, while Majendie had flown the Sunderland with the RAF.

All must have viewed the Comet as being almost impossibly modern, with its tricycle undercarriage, pressurised cabin, jet engines and swept wings! The early Comet 1s even had two Machmeters, one with an audible warning horn set to sound at Mach 0.76. But while undeniably cutting edge, the BOAC Comets were crewed like an Argonaut or Hermes, with four people on the flight deck, including Captain and co-pilot, with a radio officer behind the co-pilot, facing aft, and a navigator behind the captain, facing to port. Together, the latter pair managed the HF and VHF radios and the suite of navigation aids, which included ADF, ILS, Rebecca, and LORAN.

By the time the fifth production aircraft, G-ALYS, received the first Certificate of Airworthiness to be awarded to a Comet, on January 22, 1952 (six months ahead of

ABOVE: **The Comet looks sleek and futuristic compared to the line of cars parked outside one of London Airport's hangars.**

BELOW: **A rare colour photo of a BOAC Comet 1. G-ALYS was one of four serviceable Comets remaining following the loss of G-ALYY. Three had been lost in fatal accidents, and two had been damaged and were awaiting a decision on possible repair.** (Caz Caswell)

RIGHT: This Comet 1, G-AYLR, ran off the edge of the taxiway at Calcutta on July 25, 1953, collapsing the starboard undercarriage and badly damaging the starboard wing. Shipped back to London Airport, she never flew again.

BELOW: Comet 1 G-ALYU parked on PSP (pierced steel planking), probably at Singapore's Kallang Airport. On one occasion, a Comet taking off from Kallang found a 'bow wave' of metal sheet building up in front of the nosewheel during a take-off from an inadequately staked down PSP runway.

schedule), the Comet Unit had flown to Ahmadabad, Baghdad, Basra, Beirut, Blackbushe, Cairo, Calcutta, Delhi, Entebbe, Jakarta, Johannesburg, Karachi, Khartoum, Nicosia, Pietersburg, and Rome.

On May 2, 1952, as part of BOAC's route-proving trials, G-ALYP took off on the world's first jetliner flight to carry fare-paying passengers. The captain was Cliff Alabaster. The first passenger, officially, was Alex Henshaw, a British air racing pilot in the 1930s and a test pilot for Vickers Armstrong during World War Two. Henshaw had made a record-breaking flight to Cape Town and back in his Mew Gull, breaking the record for each leg of his flight and setting a solo record for the round trip.

The Comet flight inaugurated a scheduled service from London to Johannesburg, flying via Rome, Beirut, Khartoum, Entebbe, and finally Livingstone, in what is now Zambia. The aircraft was greeted by a crowd estimated to be 20,000 strong!

The flight took a total of 23 hours 38 minutes, though the five-stop flight from London to Johannesburg was eventually scheduled for just 21 hours and 20 minutes.

Today, the same journey is flown non-stop, and takes, on average, 10 hours and 50 minutes, but in 1952, this was astonishingly fast – and was about 50% faster than even the fastest piston-engined aircraft. The Douglas DC-6 could manage 315 mph, compared to the Comet 1's 490 mph while the Comet's faster rate of climb further reduced flight times.

And while today's airline passengers might view a day-long journey with a degree of horror, those who took that first Comet flight enjoyed 46-inch seat pitch – ten inches more than you get in Premium Economy with BA in 2022! And they had an attentive stewardess serving them drinks and nice meals on real China, and the windows beside them didn't incorporate sliding plastic shades but were instead equipped with red and white fabric curtains. And if you got bored on the Comet, you could stroll aft and avail yourself of the drinking fountain or borrow a book from the onboard library.

All that luxury didn't come cheap. At a time when the average weekly wage was then £8.68, and the average house cost £1,800, a BOAC ticket to Johannesburg cost £175

ABOVE: **Loading the mail onto a BOAC Comet 1 at London Airport. The introduction of jet airliners led to a significant improvement in air mail delivery times on some routes.**

(or £315 return), whether you flew by Comet or on a bone-shaking, ear-splitting Handley Page Hermes.

But despite the high price, demand for tickets was keen, and BOAC's Comet services to Johannesburg and Colombo were almost immediately booked solid to November.

BUSY SCHEDULE

South African flights had been increased to three per week from June, and a weekly service to Colombo had commenced in August. Services to Singapore began on October 14 and these became twice weekly from October 31. Tokyo services began in April 1953, and by August 1953 BOAC was scheduling the nine-stop London to Tokyo Comet flight for 36 hours, compared to 86 hours and 35 minutes by Argonaut.

The final Comet from BOAC's initial order, registered G-ALYZ, had begun flying in September 1952, initially carrying cargo along South American routes while simulating passenger schedules.

By the summer of 1953, BOAC's Comet fleet was operating eight long haul return services per week on four routes - three to Johannesburg, two to Tokyo, two to Singapore and one to Colombo. By then, BOAC was recording 80% load factors to Johannesburg, 81% to Singapore and 72% to Colombo. As the aircraft could be profitable with a load factor as low as 43%, the aircraft was proving as profitable as it was popular.

In their first year, BOAC's Comets had carried 30,000 passengers, including Queen Elizabeth the Queen Mother and Princess Margaret who flew a return trip from Hatfield on May 23, 1952, hosted by Sir Geoffrey and Lady de Havilland and BOAC chairman Sir Miles Thomas. With Cunningham and Buggé at the controls, the aircraft flew towards Genoa, then turned towards Bordeaux before routeing back to Hatfield. Another royal passenger was Prince Philip, who returned from the Helsinki Olympic Games on board G-ALYS on August 4, 1952, though he had already flown on the second prototype that March.

By late 1953, the Comet's star was firmly in the ascendant. The American

magazine *Popular Mechanics* judged that Britain had opened up a lead of between three and five years on the rest of the world in jet airliners. Duncan Sandys, the then Minister of Supply said that: "During the next few years the UK has an opportunity, that may not recur, of developing aircraft manufacture as one of our main export industries. On whether we grasp this opportunity and so establish firmly an industry of the utmost strategic and economic importance, our future as a great nation may depend."

Behind the scenes, de Havilland had been working hard to win export orders for the Comet. Technical observers from interested international airlines (including KLM, Air France, and Qantas) flew on the second DH106 prototype (G-5-2/G-ALZK) during its 500 hour flight test and route proving trial programme.

A bid to sell two Comet 1s to the US Overseas National Airways had failed when the US Civil Aeronautics Administration refused to accept British certification – leaving the British Aircraft Registration Board furious that its own previous acceptance of US certification of types purchased by BOAC had not been reciprocated.

Early export customers opted for the Comet 1A, an upgraded variant that could accommodate 44 passengers, with Ghost 50 Mk.2 engines uprated to 5,125 lb st, and water methanol injection allowing improved take-off performance and an increased all-up weight (115,000lb, compared to the 105,000lb of the Comet 1). Fuel capacity was increased by the installation of 856 imp gal centre bag tanks giving a total capacity of 6,909 imp gallons and increasing range by 250 miles to 1,750 miles.

Two French airlines, Union Aéromaritime de Transport and Air France, each acquired three Comet 1As, for flights to West Africa and the Middle East, with the first two aircraft for Air France taking the line positions originally reserved for ONA.

UAT began route-proving flights in December 1952 and inaugurated a Paris-Casablanca-Dakar service in February 1953. This was later extended to Abidjan, the economic capital of the Ivory Coast. A second route (Paris-Kano-Brazzaville) was inaugurated in May, and this was later extended to Johannesburg in November.

Air France flew its first commercial jet service from Le Bourget to Beirut (with a stop in Rome) on August 19, 1953.

RIGHT: **Queen Elizabeth the Queen Mother and Princess Margaret after disembarking from a Comet 1 at Hatfield, watched by Sir Geoffrey and Lady de Havilland. The Queen Mother commented that the Comet was much faster than the Queen's Flight aircraft – Vickers Vikings at the time.**

ABOVE: Interested show-goers queue to look inside a Canadian Pacific Airways Comet 1A at the 1952 Farnborough Airshow. The aircraft was destined never to enter service with Canadian Pacific, since the order was cancelled after her sister ship was lost on its delivery flight.

FIRST LOSS

On October 26, 1952, the BOAC Comet fleet suffered its first loss when G-ALYZ failed to become airborne while departing Rome's Ciampino airport and ran into rough ground at the end of the runway. Two passengers sustained minor injuries, but the aircraft was a write-off.

About four months later, on March 3, 1953, CF-CUN, a brand new Canadian Pacific Airlines Comet 1A, did much the same when attempting a night take-off from Karachi during its delivery flight to Australia. This time, however, the aircraft, named *Empress of Hawaii* ran into a dry drainage canal and then hit an embankment, bursting into flames, and killing all 11 people on board.

This was the first fatal Comet crash. Canadian Pacific cancelled its remaining Comet 1A (CF-CUM, already fully painted up and waiting delivery) which was diverted to BOAC as G-ANAV.

Both early accidents were originally attributed to pilot error, as over-rotation had led to a loss of lift from the leading edge of the aircraft's wings. It was later determined that the Comet's wing profile experienced a loss of lift at a relatively modest angle of attack, while the engine inlets also encountered a lack of pressure recovery in the same conditions. As a result, de Havilland re-profiled the wing leading edge with a pronounced 'droop', and wing fences were added to control span-wise flow and thereby reduce drag.

The second fatal Comet accident occurred on May 2, 1953, when BOAC's G-ALYV crashed in a severe thunderstorm six minutes after taking off from Calcutta's

RIGHT: Passengers walk out to a waiting Air France Comet 1A, F-BGNY. Air France's three Comet 1As were delivered in June and July 1953 and were grounded and withdrawn from service after the crash of G-ALYP in January 1954.

Dum Dum Airport, killing all 43 on board. Witnesses observed the wingless, burning Comet fuselage dive into the village of Jagalgori.

A large portion of the aircraft was recovered and reassembled at Farnborough, and it was determined that the break-up had begun with a left elevator spar failure after the aircraft encountered severe turbulence. There was some suggestion that the pilot may have inadvertently over-stressed the aircraft when pulling out of a steep dive by applying excessive forces to the fully powered flight controls. It was recommended that stricter speed limits should be observed during turbulence, and henceforth all Comets were equipped with weather radar and an artificial 'Q feel' system was introduced, which ensured that control column forces would be proportional to control loads. This was the first of its kind to be introduced in any aircraft.

Another Comet was lost on June 25, 1953, when UAT's F-BGSC skidded off the end of the runway at Dakar, Senegal, mercifully with no loss of life. Worse was to come, as is described in the next chapter, but a handful of Comet 1s and Comet 1As did return to flight after the grounding that followed the losses of G-ALYP and G-ALYY.

BOAC's four surviving Comet 1s (G-AYLS, G-AYLU, G-AYLW and G-AYLX) never flew again after late April 1954 and the airline's sole Comet 1A (G-ANAV) followed them into retirement on August 10, after flying a series of test flights in support of the accident investigation. UAT's two surviving Comet 1As (F-BGSA and F-BGSB) were similarly consigned to storage and long term scrapping, while Air France's F-BGNX was flown to Farnborough in June 1956 for fatigue testing.

COMET 1XB STANDARD

But four Comet 1A aircraft had a longer post-disaster career, after being modified to Comet 1XB standards. This saw the aircraft being modified with a strengthened fuselage, heavier gauge skins, elliptical windows, and other modifications, including 'rip-stop doublers'. The aircraft were also fitted with de Havilland Ghost 50 Mk 4 engines producing 5,500 lb st each.

Air France's F-BGNY was purchased by de Havilland in May 1954 and was modified to 1XB standards at Chester from February-September 1957. The aircraft subsequently

served at the A&AEE, Boscombe Down as XM829 from October 1958 to February 1964, when she was finally flown to Stansted for fire training.

The RCAF dispatched its Comets back to the UK for conversion to the same standards. First to arrive at Chester was 5302 on May 25, 1956 with 5301 following on July 26. The two aircraft were converted to 1XB standards between July 1956 and mid-1957 and were re-delivered to the RCAF in September 1957. The cost of the work was put at £142,000. Both RCAF Comets then served until October 3, 1963, when they were retired. The two aircraft were ferried to Mountain View on October 30, 1957, for disposal.

The last Comet 1XB was Air France's F-BGNZ, which was already at Hatfield, having been flown there for modifications on February 18, 1954. The aircraft was modified to 1XB standards at Chester, flying in its new guise on September 29, 1957. She was then registered to de Havilland Propellers as XM823 and used for various trials in support of a number of guided missile programmes, before finally being retired to RAF Shawbury on April 8, 1968, this marking the last Comet 1 flight. The aircraft can still be seen today at the RAF Museum Cosford, painted in spurious BOAC colours as G-APAS.

ABOVE: **The first UAT Comet 1A in the Aeromaritime hangar at Le Bourget. On December 23, 1953, this aircraft was 'baptised' by Jacqueline Auriol, daughter-in-law of the French President and a former holder of the women's world speed record.**

BELOW: **A Comet 1 taxies in, perhaps at Hatfield, since the aircraft in the background appears to be the second prototype, G-ALZK. Two fatal accidents in quick succession derailed the Comet 1's previously rapid progress.**

de Havilland DH.106 Comet 1
Comet 1, G-ALYS, BOAC

c/n 06005, **Fate:** Scrapped at Farnborough c.1961

G-ALYS was the world's first jet airliner to receive a certificate of airworthiness, this being awarded on January 22, 1952. It was also the first Comet delivered to BOAC, being handed over on February 4, 1952.

The BOAC Comet fleet was grounded at midnight on January 11, 1954, following the loss of G-ALYP the previous day. Some 60 modifications were made to the aircraft, including armoured panels between the engines and the pressure cabin, new smoke detectors, and fuel pipe modifications. The Comets re-entered service on 23 March 1954, all seats taken!

The disappearance of G-ALYY on Thursday April 8, just over a fortnight later, led to another grounding, and this time it was all over for the Comet 1! The type's Certificate of Airworthiness was withdrawn on April 12, and a Court of Inquiry was quickly convened.

After a relatively uneventful career by Comet 1 standards, G-ALYS was delivered to the Royal Aircraft Establishment at Farnborough in April 1954 to help with the investigation that followed the losses of G-ALYP and G-ALYY. She was one of three

BOAC Comets used in this investigation (along with G-AYLU and G-AYLW), but unusually did not end her days in the Farnborough water tank! By that time, three BOAC Comet 1s had been lost in fatal accidents, two more had been damaged beyond repair, and another was undergoing ground tests at Hatfield.

By the time she arrived at Farnborough, G-ALYS was wearing extra-large, italic '*BOAC*' titles above the cheatline - a colour scheme also seen on sister aircraft G-ALYX. The Union flag on the fin was moved up from between the tail stripes to above them, in line with the Speedbird logo.

This aircraft was badly damaged during over-fuelling tests, its lower wing skins splitting when over-filled by a Dorset bowser. The aircraft remained intact at Farnborough, sitting on its landing gear, until sometime after July 12, 1961, when it was formally struck off charge.

BELOW: **G-ALYX was a sister ship of the profile subject and was probably the only other BOAC Comet to receive these outsized titles above the cheatline. G-ALYX, the penultimate Comet 1 built, was also the penultimate Comet to stop flying, being ferried home from Cairo, unpressurised and with no passengers, on April 21, 1954.**

de Havilland DH.106 Comet 1A
Comet 1A, CF-CUM, Canadian Pacific Airlines

c/n 06013, **Fate:** Became G-ANAV with BOAC, nose at the de Havilland Aircraft Museum

Canadian Pacific Airlines was the second airline to order the Comet, announcing its purchase of two 48-seat Comet 1As on December 15, 1949. The Comet 1A was a dedicated export version of the Comet, produced to meet orders from Canadian Pacific, UAT, and Air France.

The Comet 1A had a reinforced structure, allowing an increased all up weight of 110,000lb, additional fuel capacity and increased passenger numbers. The Ghost engines featured water methanol injection, giving 10-12% greater thrust on take-off. This allowed the aircraft to operate with a higher fuel load, increasing stage lengths by as much as 20%.

The Canadian Pacific Comets wore a smart colour scheme, with a cheatline consisting of two broad stripes and a narrower pinstripe between them. A similar stripe was applied to the tail fin, above the aircraft registration.

The carrier initially planned to use its Comets between Vancouver and Hong Kong but changed its plan to one that would see the Comets flying between Sydney and Honolulu, with DC-6s flying the final leg between Honolulu and Vancouver.

The first of the pair of Comet 1As, CF-CUM, named *Empress of Vancouver*, first flew on August 10, 1952, and the second, CF-CUN *Empress of Hawaii* followed on December 24. The latter left the UK on March 2 on its delivery flight to Sydney but stalled on take-off after a refuelling stop at Karachi. The pilot selected an excessively nose-high attitude, and the aircraft failed to get airborne, overran the runway and burst into flames, killing all 11 on board.

CF-CUM remained at Hatfield for tests and was subsequently sold to BOAC as G-ANAV.

Undeterred by its bad luck, Canadian Pacific Airlines ordered three Comet 2s (with an option on a fourth) on November 16, 1953. These were intended to operate a service between Vancouver and Sydney, via San Francisco, Canton Island, Fiji, and Auckland.

The order was cancelled in the wake of the withdrawal of the Comet's Certificate of Airworthiness in 1954.

BELOW: **CF-CUN was the sister ship of the subject of this profile. Named** *Empress of Hawaii***, she was lost when she failed to become airborne during a night take-off from Karachi while on her delivery flight to Australia. From here she had been expected to open services from Sydney to Honolulu.**

de Havilland DH.106 Comet 1A
Comet 1A, F-BGSB, UAT

c/n 06016, **Fate:** Scrapped at Le Bourget

This Comet 1A was delivered to UAT (Union Aéromaritime de Transport) at Le Bourget on February 19, 1953, one of three Comets delivered to the airline - which became the second airline to operate a jet airliner.

The Comet 1A was a 44-seat export variant of the Comet 1 with a centre tank giving increased fuel capacity, higher thrust Ghost 50 Mk2 engines allowing increased all-up weight, and improved performance, including an increased cruising altitude of 40,000ft. The new variant was also ordered by Canadian Pacific, the Royal Canadian Air Force and Air France.

Union Aéromaritime de Transport was founded in 1949 by a group of technicians and the shipping line Chargeurs Réunis, the successor to the shipping company's original Aéromaritime. UAT confirmed an order for two Comet 1As on May 1, 1951, subsequently adding a third aircraft on October 30. The Comets initially served routes to West Africa, including Casablanca, Dakar, Brazzaville, Tripoli, Kano, and Abidjan and by November 1953 they were flying to Johannesburg.

The third aircraft was lost on June 25, 1953, when it overshot the runway at Dakar, fortunately with no loss of life. UAT had planned to expand its routes using three more Comet 2s, but these were cancelled, and the Comet 1As were withdrawn from service in 1954, following the crash of G-ALYY.

Urban legend has it that F-BGSB (or sister ship F-BGSA) donated its nose to the Sud Caravelle development programme. This cannot be confirmed, but the nose of the Comet and its cockpit layout were taken directly for the Caravelle!

With its bold blue and gold cheatline and French tricolour on the fin, UAT's Comet livery was the most colourful applied to early variants of the British jetliner, the airline was later 'guilty' of ushering in the fad for so-called Eurowhite colour schemes. The Eurowhite style of airline livery usually consists of an entirely white aircraft with a company logo on the tail and perhaps with a solid colour that wraps around under the rear fuselage.

BELOW: **UAT's Comet 1As were the most colourful of the early Comets, with their blue and yellow 'Harlequin' cheat lines and stylised red, white, and blue tail markings. UAT was the first export operator of the Comet 1A.**

de Havilland DH.106 Comet 1A
Comet 1A, F-BGNX, Air France

c/n 06020, **Fate:** Fuselage displayed at the de Havilland Aircraft Museum

Monsieur Max Hymans, President of Air France, announced his intention to order three Comet 1As on November 21, 1951, subject to government approval. This approval was granted, and Air France immediately started to prepare for jet services on its vital trunk routes between Paris and Cairo and Beirut, Paris and Saigon, and Paris and Dakar, Senegal.

The first Air France Comet 1A, F-BGNX, made its maiden flight on May 6, 1953, and was delivered on June 12. The second, F-BGNY, flew on May 22, and was delivered on July 7. The third, F-BGNZ, flew for the first time on March 16, 1953 and was delivered on 22 July. All were delivered in what is now remembered as Air France's 'classic' winged seahorse livery - one of the most attractive colour schemes applied to the early Comets.

F-BGNY was used to launch Air France's jet services, flying a Paris-Rome-Beirut service on August 26, 1953. More destinations soon followed, and Air France started planning for a major expansion of its Comet fleet. Unfortunately, it was not to be, and

the trio of Comet 1s were withdrawn from service following the loss of BOAC's G-ALYP near Elba and did not fly again commercially.

On the day that G-ALYY was lost, F-GBNZ was being assessed prior to planned modifications. These were cancelled, as was a planned Air France order for six Comet 2s for use on routes to South America. F-BGNX was dismantled, while the other two were modified to Comet 1XB standards and passed to the A&AEE and de Havilland Propellers. After more than 20 years on Farnborough's dump, the fuselage of F-BGNX was acquired by the de Havilland Aircraft Museum, where it was initially used for storage, but where it now remains on display, still with square windows and full Air France colours. F-BGNZ is the sole surviving intact Comet 1, albeit in 1XB configuration, and in spurious BOAC colours, exhibited in the RAF Museum at Cosford.

BELOW: **Though they only served for about six months, the three Air France Comet 1As did provide Air France with an introduction to jet operations. Two of the three aircraft were later converted to Comet 1XB standards and served with the British MOD.**

Catastrophe – The Comet Disasters of 1954

After hogging the headlines as the world's first jetliner, the Comet 1 was all too soon making headlines of exactly the wrong kind – as, in what seemed like the blink of an eye, triumph turned to tragedy.

It is hard for the modern observer to understand how the Comet was seen at the end of 1953, as it came to the end of its second year in service. Aviation was then a much riskier business, and a less risk-averse public was more tolerant of occasional fatal accidents. Aviation was much safer than it had been in the 1920s and 1930s, after all, and in any case, people accepted that there was a price to be paid for rapid technological progress.

BOAC's first Comet loss came on October 26, 1952, when G-ALYZ failed to get airborne at Rome and ploughed into the overrun. Mercifully, there were no casualties, but 'Yoke Zebra' was damaged beyond repair. The loss of G-ALYV on May 2, 1953 was a different matter, with six crew and 37 passengers losing their lives when the aircraft broke up in a tropical thunderstorm near Calcutta. The third write off hardly counts – as G-ALYR might well have been repaired, given different circumstances, but for the sake of completeness it can be noted that she suffered a taxiing accident at Calcutta on July 25, 1953, and was shipped home for possible repair.

And though BOAC had by then lost three of its nine Comet 1s (with Canadian Pacific and UAT losing two more Comet 1As in the same period – 11 dying in the CPA accident) the aircraft was literally and metaphorically riding high – representing a great source of national pride, a very obvious symbol of Britain's lead in aerospace, and a token of the progress that was coming to characterise what many described as a 'new Elizabethan age'.

And strange though it might sound, on January 10, 1954, when BOAC's longest-serving Comet broke up in mid-air and fell in pieces into the glittering Mediterranean just off the Italian island of Elba, few were seriously perturbed. Initially at least, it seemed to be just 'one of those things', and after what now looks like a rather cursory investigation, the Comet was rushed back into service.

It was only after a second catastrophic accident that the full seriousness of the situation really sank in. Before describing the nature of the problems that caused these crashes, and how they were identified, it's perhaps worth looking at what actually happened.

FLIGHT 781

BOAC Flight 781, flown by the first production Comet, G-ALYP, had originated at Kallang Airport – the first purpose-built international civil airport in Singapore, and once described as 'the finest airport in the British Empire' –

BELOW: When G-ALYP was lost on January 10, 1954, she was the highest-houred Comet then flying, with 3,681 hours recorded.

and was bound for London. The aircraft made stopovers at Don Muang Airport, Bangkok, Thailand, then at Calcutta's Dum Dum Airport, Karachi's Jinnah Airport, Muharraq in Bahrain, Beirut, and finally Rome's Ciampino airport.

Contact with the aircraft was lost some 20 minutes after take-off, as the captain, Alan Gibson, was passing a routine weather report to a BOAC Argonaut which had taken off behind it – the Argonaut captain having asked the crew of the faster-climbing Comet to report the height of the cloud-tops.

At the same moment, Italian fishermen and farmers were prompted to look upwards by three loud explosions and a thunderous roaring sound and watched horrified as debris fell from the sky – some of it reportedly ablaze.

Twenty-nine passengers and six crew died in the blink of an eye, subsequent post mortems on those recovered finding catastrophic ruptures of the lungs (the sudden decrease in cabin pressure having caused the lungs to expand until they ruptured) and skull fractures caused as the passengers were thrown out of their seats and propelled violently head-first into the cabin roof as the aircraft 'bunted' as it broke up. Ten of the 29 passengers were children or teenagers, and the casualties included Chester Wilmot, a prominent Australian journalist and military historian working for the BBC, and Dorothy Beecher Baker, a prominent member of the Bahá'í Faith.

Sir Miles Thomas, BOAC's chairman, announced a temporary suspension of Comet services: "as a measure of prudence to enable a minute and unhurried technical examination of every aircraft in the Comet fleet to be carried out at maintenance headquarters at London

airport." The carrier's remaining Comets underwent in-depth inspections, while Air France and Union Aéro Maritime des Transports (the two French airlines equipped with the Comet) also suspended their Comet services.

Plans were also made to recover the wreckage of G-AYLP. In the meantime, an expert panel, the Abell Committee, was set up to investigate the causes of the accident. The panel was convened under the leadership of Charles Abell, BOAC's deputy operations director for engineering, and included representatives from de Havilland, the Air Registration Board and the Ministry of Transport and Civil Aviation's Accident Investigation Branch.

The Committee examined a number of potential causes of the accident, ranging from flutter of the control surfaces to failure of the flight controls or primary structure. Sabotage was ruled out, as there was no evidence of explosive residue on any of the recovered wreckage or bodies. Failure of the cabin was felt to be unlikely, given the extensive testing by de Havilland (which simulated 18,000 pressurisation cycles), and the committee settled on fire as the most likely explanation, and so fire prevention and suppression was the focus of the package of precautionary modifications that the committee recommended, though some modifications were also made to prevent cracking of the wings. No actual fault had been found in the aircraft (though the forensic reconstruction of the wreckage had only just begun when the Abell Committee reported its findings), and the British government decided against

ABOVE: G-ALYP is seen here during an early test flight, with an unpainted replacement rear passenger door fitted.

LEFT: G-ALYP was en route home from Rome when she was lost, having set off from Singapore, and having previously stopped in Karachi, Bahrain, and Beirut.

BELOW: G-ALYP was the first production Comet 1 and had flown the world's first commercial jet airliner service just 18 months before the tragic accident that destroyed her.

RIGHT: Though little wreckage was recovered from the loss of G-ALYY on April 8, 1954, the close similarities between the two accidents told their own story.

BELOW: The wreckage of G-ALYP was taken to Farnborough and carefully reassembled. Damage from immersion in sea water and from the salvage process was reportedly slight. The investigators soon focused their attention on the twin ADF antenna 'windows' on the fuselage spine (see inset).

opening a further public inquiry into the accident. The financial impact of the aircraft's grounding on BOAC's operations had been considerable, and there was a real desire not to do anything that might diminish the reputation of the British aerospace industry.

Sir Miles Thomas forwarded the Abell report to the government on February 19, expressing his view that there was 'no reason why passenger services should not be resumed', and saying that: "We obviously wouldn't be flying the Comet with passengers if we weren't satisfied conditions were suitable." Lord Brabazon, chairman of the ARB, agreed with Sir Miles, and Sir Frederick Bowhill, chairman of the Air Safety Board, recommended that the Comet should return to service once the modifications had been incorporated. Alan Lennox-Boyd, Minister of Transport and Civil Aviation, therefore, gave permission for Comet operations to resume from March 23.

FLIGHT 201

But two weeks later, on April 8, 1954, the same thing happened again. This time G-ALYY, operating as South African Airways Flight 201 from London to Johannesburg, crashed into the Mediterranean after taking off from Ciampino, killing the 14 passengers and seven crew.

'Yoke Yoke' was being chartered from BOAC by South African Airways, with a South African crew and was on the second stage of its flight from London to Johannesburg.

Flight 201 had taken off from London the previous day, under the command of captain William Mostert, arriving at Rome approximately two and a half hours later. On arrival at Rome, engineers discovered some minor faults, including a faulty fuel gauge and 30 loose bolts on the left wing, and this delayed the aircraft's departure for Cairo by 25 hours.

The aircraft finally took off for Cairo at 1832hrs GMT and rapidly climbed towards its planned cruising height of 35,000ft. The weather was good, but the sky was overcast. The crew reported overhead the Ostia beacon at 1837hrs, passing through the altitude of 7,000ft.

'Yoke Yoke' reported climbing through 11,600ft at Ponza at 1849hrs and reported passing abeam of Naples at 1857hrs. At 1907hrs the crew contacted Cairo on the long range HF radio and reported an ETA of 2102hrs. This was the last message received from 'Yoke Yoke', which disintegrated as it reached around 35,000ft, killing everyone on board.

After repeated unsuccessful attempts by both Cairo and Rome air traffic control to contact the aircraft, there was a dawning realisation that another Comet had been lost. The Italian air-sea rescue services were notified, and an intensive search began at dawn the next day, the Royal Navy aircraft carrier HMS *Eagle* and the destroyer HMS *Daring* subsequently joining the search.

Later that day, a BEA Airspeed Ambassador aircraft reported spotting an oil patch and bodies and wreckage in the water some 70 miles south of Naples, and about 30 miles

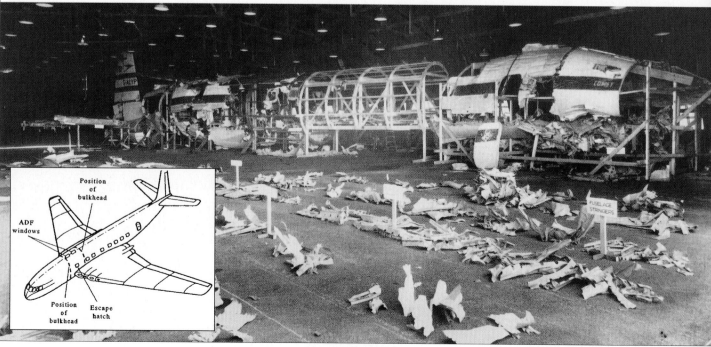
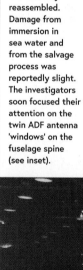

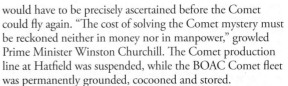

ABOVE AND LEFT:
The main portion
of fuselage
containing the ADF
'windows' is today
in the Science
Museum collection,
though it is no
longer on public
display. The author
hopes it could
be transferred to
the de Havilland
Aircraft Museum,
to be displayed
alongside the other
Comet exhibits.
The dark rectangles
are holes where
metal was removed
for metallurgical
analysis.

BELOW LEFT AND
BELOW RIGHT: The
fatigue failure that
led to the loss
of G-ALYP was
suspected to have
originated at the
top right corner of
the ADF window
seen here.

northeast of Stromboli. Five or six bodies (reports vary) and some small items of floating wreckage were recovered.

This new and unexplained Comet crash (the second in just three months) had come less than three weeks after the type had been thoroughly inspected, and then modified and returned to commercial service after a ten-week grounding following the previous Comet crash on January 10.

BOAC immediately and voluntarily grounded all of its Comets as it had done three months before, but this time, Alan Tindal Lennox-Boyd, the minister of transport, withdrew the Comet's Certificate of Airworthiness on April 9, 'pending further detailed investigations into the causes of the recent disasters'. A downbeat Sir Miles Thomas, BOAC's chairman, said that the accident represented: "a very great tragedy and a major setback for British civil aviation."

This time it was not just 'one of those things' and word came down from on high that the cause of the accidents would have to be precisely ascertained before the Comet could fly again. "The cost of solving the Comet mystery must be reckoned neither in money nor in manpower," growled Prime Minister Winston Churchill. The Comet production line at Hatfield was suspended, while the BOAC Comet fleet was permanently grounded, cocooned and stored.

UAT grounded its Comet 1As on April 12, (Air France having grounded its aircraft on January 11, after the loss of G-ALYP), and the Royal Canadian Air Force quickly did the same.

Of the remaining BOAC aircraft, G-AYLS was delivered to Farnborough for testing, as was G-ALYU, the latter after a final flight to Hatfield on April 10. Meanwhile G-ALYX, which had been marooned at Cairo with a minor fault when the type's Certificate of Airworthiness was withdrawn, finally flew home, unpressurised and with no passengers, on April 21. G-ALYW followed from Colombo on April 27.

The former Canadian Pacific Airlines Comet 1A, now registered G-ANAV, was BOAC's lowest-houred aircraft, and was flown to Farnborough on May 3 for flight trials in support of the accident investigation. The aircraft flew 50 sorties, the final one occurring on 10 August.

The Comet 2X prototype, G-AYLT continued flying, unpressurised, on engine development work, but was withdrawn from flying use on June 22. The other flying Comet 2s (G-AMXA, G-AMXB, and G-AMXC) were temporarily grounded.

There was an urgent need to get to the bottom of the two Comet accidents, but it was clear that, given the technology available at the time, it would not be possible to examine both sets of wreckage to the degree required. The depth of the Mediterranean Sea at the location of the second crash meant that a salvage mission to recover the remains of G-ALYY would be impractical. But since the circumstances surrounding the crash of G-ALYP were so similar, it was felt that if the cause of the loss of 'Yoke Peter' could be found, it would also explain the loss of the second aircraft.

The investigation into the crash of G-ALYP (BOAC Flight 781) was still in progress when G-ALYY (SAA Flight 201) was lost, and it was decided that a joint investigation would be appropriate. Thus, on October 19, 1954, the Cohen Committee was established to examine the causes of the Comet crashes.

The committee, chaired by a senior judge Lord Lionel Cohen, tasked an investigation team led by Sir Arnold Hall, director of the Royal Aircraft Establishment (RAE) at Farnborough, to perform a more-detailed accident investigation.

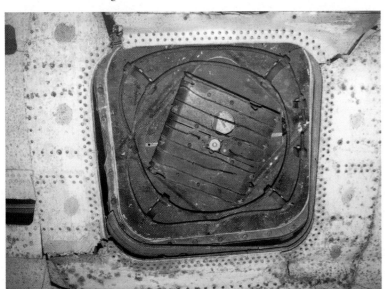

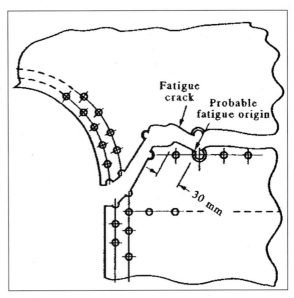

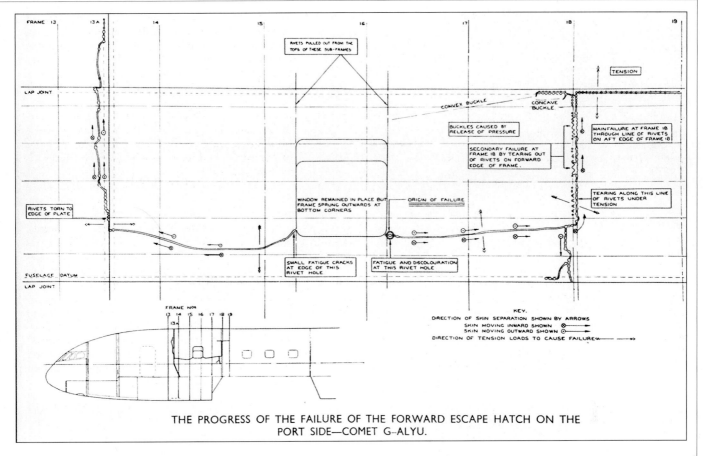

FRAME 13 | 13A | 14 | 15 | 16 | 17 | 18 | 19

RIVETS PULLED OUT FROM THE TOPS OF THESE SUB-FRAMES

TENSION

LAP JOINT

CONVEX BUCKLE | CONCAVE BUCKLE

BUCKLES CAUSED BY RELEASE OF PRESSURE

MAINFAILURE AT FRAME 18 THROUGH LINE OF RIVETS ON AFT EDGE OF FRAME 18

SECONDARY FAILURE AT FRAME 18 BY TEARING OUT OF RIVETS ON FORWARD EDGE OF FRAME.

RIVETS TORN TO EDGE OF PLATE

TEARING ALONG THIS LINE OF RIVETS UNDER TENSION

WINDOW REMAINED IN PLACE BUT FRAME SPRUNG OUTWARDS AT BOTTOM CORNERS | ORIGIN OF FAILURE

FUSELAGE DATUM
LAP JOINT

SMALL FATIGUE CRACKS AT EDGE OF THIS RIVET HOLE | FATIGUE AND DISCOLOURATION AT THIS RIVET HOLE

FRAME Nos
13 14 15 16 17 18 19
13A

KEY.
DIRECTION OF SKIN SEPARATION SHOWN BY ARROWS
SKIN MOVING INWARD SHOWN
SKIN MOVING OUTWARD SHOWN
DIRECTION OF TENSION LOADS TO CAUSE FAILURE

THE PROGRESS OF THE FAILURE OF THE FORWARD ESCAPE HATCH ON THE PORT SIDE—COMET G-ALYU.

Investigators were able to conclude that the crash of G-ALYP had been due to failure of the pressure cabin at the forward ADF antenna aperture in the cabin roof. These window-like apertures contained opaque fibreglass panels covering aerials for the ADF navigation system. The recovered fuselage roof section of G-ALYP containing the two ADF 'windows', was on display in the Science Museum in London for many years but is now in store.

In June 1956, some more wreckage from G-ALYP was accidentally trawled up from an area about 15 miles south of where the original wreckage had been found. This wreckage was from the starboard side of the cabin just above the three front windows. Subsequent examination at Farnborough suggested that the primary failure was probably near to this area rather than at the rear automatic direction finding window on the roof of the cabin, as had been previously thought. These findings were kept secret until the details were published in 2015.

In addition, it was discovered that the stresses around pressure cabin apertures were considerably higher than had been anticipated, particularly around sharp-cornered cut-outs, such as square windows. As a result, future jet airliners would feature windows with rounded corners, the purpose of the curve being to eliminate a stress concentration. This was a noticeable distinguishing feature of all later models of the Comet.

ABOVE: An eight foot split occurred in the forward fuselage after 3,057 pressurised flights – 1,826 of them simulated in the water tank. The damaged section was then replaced to allow testing to continue, and after 5,410 flights fatigue cracks appeared in the wheel wells. After that, a 15ft split occurred in the rear fuselage.

BELOW LEFT AND BELOW RIGHT: G-ANAV underwent water tank tests in 1955, resulting in the fuselage splitting along almost the entire length of the pressure cabin.

Stress around the window corners was found to be much higher than expected and stresses on the skin were generally more than previously expected or tested. The windows' square shape caused stress concentration by generating levels of stress two or three times greater than across the rest of the fuselage.

In 2012 a finite element analysis was conducted to find the stress values in a digital model of the Comet's cabin window loaded to a pressure differential of 8.25psi. In this model, the maximum stress level at the margin of one of the outer rows of rivet holes near the corner of the window was almost five times greater than in the areas of skin remote from the windows.

The possibility of a failure of the pressure cabin had been considered and initially rejected as the Comet's cabin had been designed to a much higher strength than was considered necessary at the time. British Civil Airworthiness Requirements (BCAR) had required a safety factor of 1.33 times P (with P being the cabin's 'Proof' pressure), with an ultimate load of 2 times P, but the safety factor used in the Comet was 2.5 times P. Manufacturers de Havilland had tested a prototype fuselage to a safety factor between 1 and 2 approximately 30 times without a problem, then tested up to design pressure 16,000 times to guard against fatigue. Since the design life was 10,000 cycles, this seemed satisfactory. Unfortunately, the company

de Havilland Comet

did their fatigue testing on a fuselage that had been pre-stressed to a factor 2 safety margin, which had actually changed the properties of the metal, actually (and counter-intuitively) making it more resistant to fatigue. The pre-stressed material was thereby able to withstand 16,000 cycles whereas the ordinary metal without pre-stressing failed at nearer to 1,000 cycles.

To find out what had caused the first failure, the entire fuselage of Comet 1 G-ALYU was placed into a specially-built Braithwaite water tank. This allowed the cabin to be repeatedly pressurised and depressurised with water (allowing it to fail representatively, but not explosively) while the protruding wings were subjected to simulated flight loads using hydraulic rams. The experiment was run around the clock, seven days per week.

On June 24, 1954, after 3,057 flight cycles (1,221 actual and 1,836 simulated), G-ALYU's fuselage burst open at a bolt hole, forward of the forward left escape hatch. The failure then propagated longitudinally along a fuselage stringer at the widest point of the fuselage and the fuselage frames did not have sufficient strength to prevent the crack from spreading.

The fuselage of G-ALYU had failed after a number of cycles that represented roughly three times that completed

by G-ALYP at the time of the accident, but it was still much earlier than anyone had expected, and based on these findings, it was calculated that Comet 1 structural failures could be expected at anywhere from 1,000 to 9,000 cycles. G-ALYP had made 1,290 pressurised flights when lost, while G-ALYY had made just 900 pressurised flights.

The failure was found to be a result of metal fatigue caused by the repeated pressurisation and depressurisation of the aircraft cabin. An aggravating factor was that the supports around the windows were riveted, not riveted and glued, as the original specifications for the aircraft had called for. The problem was further exacerbated by the punch rivet construction technique employed by de Havilland. Unlike drill riveting, the imperfect nature of the hole created by punch riveting could cause fatigue cracks to start developing around the rivet.

The Cohen enquiry closed on November 24, 1954, having "found that the basic design of the Comet was sound" and made no observations or recommendations regarding the shape of the windows.

The official document of findings was released by the Ministry of Transport and Civil Aviation on February 1, 1955. The conclusion was that a combination of design defects, construction flaws and metal fatigue were the likely explanation for the explosive decompression that caused both accidents.

In its response to the report de Havilland stated: "Now that the danger of high level fatigue in pressure cabins has been generally appreciated, de Havilland will take adequate measures to deal with this problem. To this end we propose to use thicker gauge materials in the pressure cabin area and to strengthen and redesign windows and cut outs and so lower the general stress to a level at which local stress concentrations either at rivets and bolt holes or as such may occur by reason of cracks caused accidentally during manufacture or subsequently, will not constitute a danger."

The Comet programme was back on, while the enquiry led to improved design techniques, new accident investigation procedures, and revised estimates for the strength requirements of airliner pressure cabins. Henceforth, aircraft were designed to 'Fail safe' or 'Safe Life' standards, though catastrophic fatigue failures have continued to occur.

LEFT: The Rt Hon Sir Hartley Shawcross QC, MP, represented the de Havilland Aircraft Company at the enquiry. Shawcross was the former attorney general in Clement Attlee's Labour government and had been the lead British prosecutor at the Nuremberg War Crimes tribunal, as well as Britain's principal delegate to the United Nations.

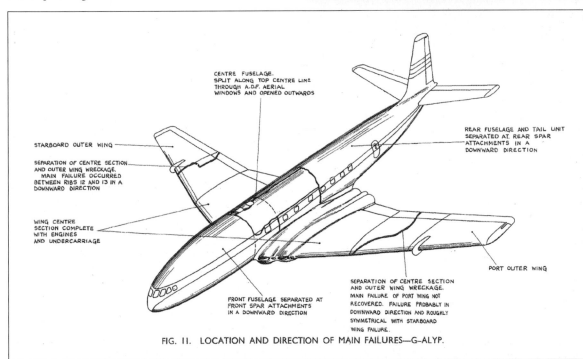

LEFT: A contemporary diagram illustrating the break-up of G-ALYP.

CENTRE FUSELAGE. SPLIT ALONG TOP CENTRE LINE THROUGH A.D.F. AERIAL WINDOWS AND OPENED OUTWARDS

STARBOARD OUTER WING

SEPARATION OF CENTRE SECTION AND OUTER WING WRECKAGE. MAIN FAILURE OCCURRED BETWEEN RIBS 12 AND 13 IN A DOWNWARD DIRECTION

WING CENTRE SECTION COMPLETE WITH ENGINES AND UNDERCARRIAGE

REAR FUSELAGE AND TAIL UNIT SEPARATED AT REAR SPAR ATTACHMENTS IN A DOWNWARD DIRECTION

PORT OUTER WING

FRONT FUSELAGE SEPARATED AT FRONT SPAR ATTACHMENTS IN A DOWNWARD DIRECTION

SEPARATION OF CENTRE SECTION AND OUTER WING WRECKAGE. MAIN FAILURE OF PORT WING NOT RECOVERED. FAILURE PROBABLY IN DOWNWARD DIRECTION AND ROUGHLY SYMMETRICAL WITH STARBOARD WING FAILURE.

FIG. II. LOCATION AND DIRECTION OF MAIN FAILURES—G-ALYP.

LEFT: Comet fuselage sections cocooned at Farnborough in 1970, where they had been put in storage for possible use in tests associated with the Comet enquiry. Left to right are F-BGNX (now in the de Havilland Aircraft Museum), G-ALYW (converted to become a Nimrod travelling exhibit) and the first prototype G-ALVG. (Chris Martin)

de Havilland DH.106 Comet 1
Comet 1, G-ALYP, BOAC

c/n 06003, **Fate:** Written off in air accident, January 10, 1954. 35 killed

The loss of the first production Comet 1 on January 10, 1954, revealed the Comet 1's fatal flaw – a terrible susceptibility to metal fatigue around the square-shaped windows and ADF antenna cut-outs. G-ALYP had inaugurated BOAC jet services on May 2, 1952, operating from London to Rome, Beirut, Cairo, Khartoum, Entebbe, and Livingstone, before finally arriving at Palmietfontein, Johannesburg on May 3, 1952.

The aircraft made its final flight from Ciampino, bound for London – the last leg of a service from Singapore to London.

The last radio transmission from callsign 'Yoke Peter' broke off abruptly, about 19 minutes after take-off, as captain Gibson started asking a BOAC Argonaut if its captain had received the Comet's previous report of passing the cloud tops. Witnesses reported three explosions before wreckage was seen falling into the sea, at least one major section in flames.

BOAC grounded the Comet fleet for inspection and a package of modifications, focused mainly on the incorrect assumption that a catastrophic fire was the most likely cause of the accident. It was only after the subsequent loss of G-ALYY, and extensive testing, that the true cause became apparent.

Ground tests had previously indicated that the fuselage should withstand up to 18,000 pressurisation cycles, and no in-service Comet had come close to that total, so the discovery of a fatigue problem came as a terrible shock. G-ALYP herself had completed just 1,290 flights, totalling 3,681 flying hours.

Services were therefore resumed on March 23, 1954, and BOAC decided to order five Comet 3s for use on the Transatlantic route, signing a contract on February 1, 1954. The airline enjoyed just over two months of Comet 1 operations before fate again intervened.

The aircraft wears the standard BOAC colour scheme of the time, with a white tail and white fuselage top, and a dark blue cheatline outlined in gold separating the white topsides and highly polished under-surfaces. This tapered to a point in front of the cockpit.

BELOW: **G-ALYP, often known by the last two letters of its callsign, 'Yoke Peter', had made a heavy landing at Khartoum in August 1952, damaging the landing gear and flaps, but this did not have any bearing on her loss on January 10, 1954.**

de Havilland DH.106 Comet 1
Comet 1, G-ALYY, BOAC/SAA

c/n 060011, **Fate:** Written off in air accident, April 8, 1954. 21 killed

The straw that broke the Comet 1's reputation for good was the loss of this BOAC/SAA Comet 1, G-ALYY. Callsign 'Yoke Yoke' was lost on April 8, 1954 while en route to South Africa, operated by an SAA crew, and flying as SA 201. The aircraft left Rome-Ciampino Airport at 19:32 local, bound for Cairo, carrying a crew of seven, and 14 passengers. About half an hour later, while cruising at an estimated altitude of 35,000 feet, the aircraft disappeared from radar screens and crashed into the Tyrrhenian Sea, about 17km off the Italian coast, close to the island of Stromboli.

About 70% of the aircraft was recovered and reconstructed at Farnborough. The engines were recovered more or less intact, showing that engine disintegration was not the cause of the accident, and neither was any evidence of fire found.

The official investigation stated that it was "unable to form a definite opinion on the cause of the accident near Naples," due to the absence of wreckage, but said that it wanted to "draw attention to the fact that the explanation offered for the accident at Elba appears to be applicable to that at Naples."

The Comet 1 and South Africa were inextricably linked. When BOAC began the world's first jet passenger service on May 2, 1952 it was on the London to Johannesburg route. This meant that the jet age arrived in South Africa the next day, on May 3, 1952, when the BOAC de Havilland Comet arrived in Palmietfontein after its 24-hour journey from England, which had included five refuelling stops en route. South African Airways (SAA) began charter services on the Springbok route between Johannesburg and London on October 3, 1953, and two BOAC Comets were painted in a hybrid colour scheme, with SAA logos added to the nose and tail, and these were operated by South African crews. One of these two aircraft, Comet 1A G-ANAV, opened the new service between London and Johannesburg.

BELOW: **When lost on April 8, 1954, G-ALYY, the subject of the profile above, was wearing both BOAC and South African Airways markings, like her sister aircraft, Comet 1A G-ANAV, seen in this evocative photograph.**

A Comet Cut Short

Work had commenced on the Comet 2 even before the first version had been grounded. However, the fate of the Comet 1 meant that the new variant didn't enter commercial service.

By the time G-ALYP made its historic flight to Johannesburg on May 2, 1952, the Comet 1 was already being viewed as an interim type. Sir Miles Thomas, BOAC's chairman believed that the new jets would stimulate a massive growth in airline traffic and passenger numbers, and confidently predicted tourist services "which will girdle the earth."

To provide these new services, especially on the North Atlantic, where demand for tourist class flights was already booming, de Havilland developed the Comet 2.

The new type was to use the 6,500lb st Rolls Royce Avon – an axial flow turbojet engine already in production for a range of military types, including the Canberra, Swift, and Hunter. The new engine promised better take-off

RIGHT: Initially flown without any airline 'branding', the Comet 2X did eventually gain a BOAC livery for route proving flights in the Summer of 1953. These took the aircraft to Entebbe in East Africa, and to Latin America.

performance, 14% more payload and longer range, and the Comet 2 soon attracted interest from a range of potential export customers, including British Commonwealth Pacific Airlines, Eastern Airlines, Japan Air Lines, Linea Aerospatial Venezolana, National Airlines, and Panair do Brasil.

The sixth Comet built, G-ALYT, was fitted with Avons and served as the Comet 2X, a prototype of sorts for the new variant, though it lacked the definitive production Comet 2's 36in fuselage extension. It flew for the first time on February 16, 1952, by which time 24 examples of the new Comet 2 were on order, including 12 for BOAC.

When the loss of two BOAC Comet 1s finally grounded the fleet, all remaining Comet 1s and Comet 1As were withdrawn from service, and all outstanding airline orders for the Comet 2 were cancelled. A planned programme to produce a Comet 2 variant with more powerful Avon engines was delayed.

With the cause of the disasters found to be metal fatigue, it was clear that the Comet would require a significant redesign of its fuselage, and that any existing aircraft would need significant modifications.

De Havilland was left with an estimated £15m worth of unsalable aircraft, useless jigs, and tools (more than £385m in 2022 terms) and faced possible bankruptcy. In response, the Cabinet authorised a rescue package In order to 'safeguard the public interest in the Comet and other projects'. This would eventually amount to some £10m (£256m today) including direct monetary assistance to ease the firm's cashflow as well as orders for Comet 2s for the RAF.

Most of the Comet 2s that were still on the production line were given a package of modifications similar to the one that created the Comet 1XB, with oval windows, increased skin thickness and rip-stop doublers. Interestingly, the elliptical windows were not designed in direct response to the loss of G-ALYP and G-ALYY, and had already been adopted for the Comet 3, before the 'Comet disasters'.

Three Comet 2s (plus the Comet 2X prototype) had already flown in their original unmodified form, and two more were in too advanced a stage of construction to be easily modified.

G-AMXA had flown for the first time on August 27, 1953, and had been delivered to BOAC on January 21, 1954, while G-AMXB and G-AMXC had flown in November 1953. G-AMXD followed on August 20, 1954.

With an urgent RAF requirement for three Comet SIGINT aircraft, G-AMXA, G-AMXC and G-AMXE were flown to Marshalls of Cambridge for conversion to Comet 2R standards, becoming XK655, XK659 and XK663, respectively. Since the Comet 2Rs would have large

apertures cut into their pressure cabins for new antennas, it was decided that they would be flown unpressurised, and their square windows were therefore retained, though they did receive other modifications.

G-AMXB became the flying prototype for the new RAF transport variant, receiving the full 'anti fatigue' modifications.

G-AMXD was initially flown unpressurised, undertaking hot and high trials from Khartoum and Entebbe. She was later fully modified while being converted to Comet 2E standards, with Avon 524 engines in her outer nacelles. G-AMXK was built to Comet 2E standards, and both aircraft were briefly used by BOAC for testing and route-proving for the new Comet 4 from August 1957 until June 1958. Both then became experimental aircraft, and thereafter, the Comet 2 was a purely military aircraft, whose story is told in the chapter 'In Uniform' starting on page 80.

Some 14 Comet 2s were built at Hatfield, with one more completed and used for fatigue testing, and seven more remaining incomplete.

One more Comet 2 (originally laid down for UAT) was built at Chester and was completed for the RAF as XK716. Four more Chester-built airframes remained incomplete, and were scrapped, and 11 more were cancelled.

Shorts of Belfast completed two Comet 2 fuselages, and these were eventually shipped to Chester, where they were eventually scrapped.

ABOVE: **The first true Comet 2 was the 23rd Comet, G-AMXA, which followed two prototypes, nine production Comet 1s, ten Comet 1As and the Comet 2X. G-AMXA was subsequently converted to become a Comet 2R SIGINT aircraft for the Royal Air Force, serving in that guise until 1974.**

BELOW: **This aircraft, G-AMXK, was modified on the production line to become a Comet 2E, with more powerful Avon RA.29 engines in the outboard nacelles. She was used by BOAC for Comet 4 route-proving and training.**

de Havilland DH.106 Comet 2
Comet 2, G-AMXD, BOAC

c/n 06026, **Fate:** Became Comet 2E XN453 with the RAE, retired February 1973 and scrapped

Though delivered in BOAC colours, Comet 2 G-AMXD never served with the airline. The aircraft was built for BOAC but was not taken up. G-AMXD made its maiden flight on August 20, 1954, in the hands of Pat Fillingham, and was then used for testing in support of the RAF's Comet C.Mk 2.

Compared to the Comet 1, the Comet 2 had a stretched fuselage, and modified, drooped leading edges, and was powered by four Avon RA.25 Mk 503/504 engines. It retained the increased fuel capacity of the Comet 1A, and the new Avon engines gave a useful boost in performance and range. Some 22 Comet 2s were built to meet a BOAC requirement for 11 of the new version, British Commonwealth Pacific Airways (who wanted six), Japan Air Lines (two), CPA, UAT, Air France and Panair do Brasil, but the type never entered airline service as orders were cancelled following the Comet 1 crashes and the subsequent grounding.

Three aircraft had already flown, and eventually 16 were completed, one as a structural test airframe, 13 of them for the Royal Air Force. The other two (G-AMXD, seen here, and G-AMXK) were converted to Comet 2E standards, serving as testbeds for the Avon RA.29 Mk 524 engines selected for the Comet 4. The new engines were fitted in the outboard nacelles, which had new Comet 4 type large area intakes fitted.

The two Comet 2Es operated with a so-called 'Comet Flight' within BOAC, which aimed to speed Avon development, and to allow crew training to get underway. The two aircraft were later used extensively for testing and evaluation of the Decca/Dectra navigation system that was also planned for the transatlantic Comet 4s.

G-AMXD was returned to the Ministry of Supply in May 1958, and (as XN453) joined the Royal Aircraft Establishment, at Farnborough for 'radio development' work on May 1, 1959. The aircraft made its final flight on February 9, 1973, and ended up on Farnborough's fire dump, its remains finally being cleared in 1986.

BELOW: **G-AMXD shows off the different intake shapes for the Comet 2 (inboard) and Comet 4 (outboard) sometime after her conversion to Comet 2E standards in 1957. The aircraft gained a host of structural modifications at the same time, including elliptical windows.**

de Havilland DH.106 Comet 2E, XV144 (c/n 06033), Blind Landing Experimental Unit, RAE Bedford

de Havilland DH.106 Comet 2E
Comet 2E, XV144, BLEU

c/n 06033, **Fate:** Retired in June 1971. Scrapped

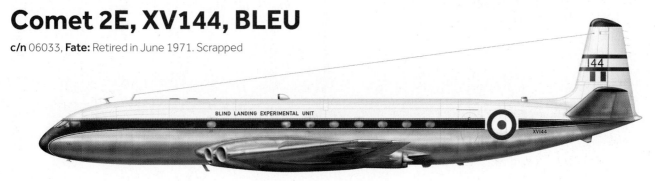

This Comet was one of 16 Comet 2s built, one of which served only as a structural test aircraft, and 13 of which were converted to Comet C.Mk 2, T.Mk 2 and R.Mk 2 (or 2R) standards. This aircraft (then registered G-AMXK) was one of the remaining pair, alongside Comet 2, G-AMXD (c/n 06026), shown on page 34. These aircraft were both converted to Comet 2E standards, with Avon RA.29 Mk 524 engines in the outboard nacelles, and with new Comet 4 type large area intakes fitted outboard. As such, painted in full BOAC colours, the aircraft were used for Comet 4 development flying from July 1957.

Operating with BOAC's Comet Flight, the two Comet 2Es were used for training, route-proving, and trials of the Decca Dectra navigation system.

After the completion of test flying in support of the Comet 4 programme, in early 1958, G-AMXD was returned to the Ministry of Supply. BOAC then switched G-AMXK to transatlantic proving flights to gain 423 further flying hours of valuable operational experience on the North Atlantic route.

G-AMXK then spent six years allocated to Smiths Instruments for Autoland trials, based mainly at Hatfield, before being delivered to the Blind Landing Experimental Unit (BLEU) at the Royal Aircraft Establishment Bedford in November 1966,

with the new military serial XV144 and RAF roundels and fin flashes applied over the previous Smiths Industries livery.

This consisted of silver-painted under-surfaces, with a white fuselage top and tail fin, divided by a broad dark blue cheatline, with fine pinstripes above and below. The 'last three' of the serial was carried between two broad blue bands on the tail fin.

The aircraft was formally allocated to RAE Farnborough for spares recovery on June 21, 1971, having flown there five days earlier. Placed on the dump at Farnborough in 1973, the aircraft was finally scrapped in 1975, having served mainly as a spares source for her sistership, Comet 2E XN453 (previously G-AMXD).

RIGHT AND BELOW: The two Comet 2Es ended up side by side on Farnborough's scrap dump, XV144's final role having been to provide spares for XN453, which flew on for about two years after '144's retirement. (Chris England)

The Trail-blazing Comet 3

The Comet 3 provided a stepping stone between the troubled early Comets and the later and more successful Comet 4s, but also functioned as a prototype, speeding development of the later versions. There was just one aircraft, but boy! What an aircraft it was...

The Comet 3 is remembered as the aircraft that bridged the gap between the early short-fuselage variants, and the later, 'definitive' Comet 4, though when launched it was itself intended to be the ultimate Comet.

De Havilland's plan had been for there to be a two-variant Comet family – both versions to be powered by the new Rolls Royce Avon, with the smaller Comet 2 serving shorter-range and 'thinner' routes (though it would also be capable of flying to New York), and the long range Comet 3 flying more passengers non-stop across the Atlantic.

This seemed to be a winning proposition. Jet services across the Atlantic were a 'holy grail' to airline operators, and while the Comet 1 and 2 had been greeted with indifference by the US airline industry, the Comet 3 had an entirely different effect.

The appearance of the Comet 1 had not been enough to tempt Boeing's president, Bill Allen, to admit that he was doing any more than 'reviewing' plans for a jet airliner – privately he opined that to do so might risk pouring millions of dollars down the drain. Meanwhile, Douglas continued to work on its piston-engined DC-7C, whose prototype

would not fly until May 18, 1953, and Lockheed's idea of a futuristic airliner was the L-1649 Starliner, a derivative of the pre-war Constellation! The threat of competition from the Comet 1 clearly ruffled few feathers!

But watching the unfolding success of BOAC's Comet 1, together with rumours of the Comet 3 was probably what changed Bill Allen's mind about jet airliners, turning him from sceptic to convert. It certainly prompted him to invest company money in the launch of the Model 367-80 (the forerunner of the Boeing 707) on May 20, 1952.

The Comet 3 was officially announced at Farnborough in September 1952 (though work had been underway for some months), and in October the new type received its first order, from Pan American World Airways. Pan Am was then America's principal and largest international air carrier and unofficial overseas 'flag carrier'. *Time Magazine* reported that the order, for three Comet 3s and seven options, for delivery in 1957, had "surprised and dismayed the American aircraft industry." It probably surprised BOAC, too, whose own order for three Comet 3s followed a year later, joining Air India, which had signed for two Comet 3s in May 1953.

BELOW: De Havilland envisaged the Comet 2 (represented here by G-AMXD, furthest from the camera) and the Comet 3 as being complementary, together providing airline customers with everything they might need. Alas, it was not to be!

LEFT: The Comet 3 prototype began its career wearing this anonymous-looking colour scheme, based on the BOAC livery, but without titles, logos, or other branding. It soon gave way to a version of the BOAC colours based on that applied to the corporation's Comet 1s.

ENHANCEMENTS

The Comet 3 was an altogether larger aircraft than the Comet 2. The fuselage was 15 feet and 5 inches longer (at 111 ft 6 in), with room for 56 to 76 passengers, depending on configuration. The Comet 3's fuselage was divided into two compartments separated by a bulkhead and could have been separated into two classes with 26-34 seats in the front compartment and 32-42 in the rear. The extended fuselage also gave greater storage capacity with a 150ft³ hold under the forward floor, and 240ft³ under the rear floor, with a further 155ft³ compartment at the extreme end of the pressure hull.

The Comet 3 introduced a new de Havilland double chair. This weighed only 50lb but offered first class comfort, and each seat was individually adjustable and also incorporated a leg rest attachment for use at night.

The aircraft was powered by a more advanced version of the Rolls-Royce Avon engine (the RA26 Mk 502), with annular ring combustion chambers, producing 10,000lb of thrust from each engine (up from 7,300lb on the definitive Comet 2 powerplant).

The Comet 3 carried 20% more fuel (10,000 imperial gallons) than previous variants, thanks in part to the addition of pinion fuel tanks on the wing leading edge. The wing itself also marked a major change by comparison with earlier variants.

A major wing modification was assessed on the original Comet 1 prototype, G-ALVG, in late 1952, before the Comet 3 specification had been finally defined. This introduced what was sometimes referred to as the 'full soft-pencil' change of leading edge profile. This extended well beyond the front spar and also incorporated dummy wing pod tanks (with a notional 400 gallon capacity). A large wind-tunnel model was mounted

in the low-speed wind-tunnel to allow detailed testing alongside the full scale tests. This testing achieved a high standard of free-air stall handling which carried over to the Comet 3 which used the new wing profile.

The all up weight was 150,000lb, allowing a full payload of 20,000lb on stage lengths of up to 2,400 miles (or 60% greater than the Comet 1). With a lower payload of 17,350lb the Comet 3 could fly stage lengths of 2,600 miles.

Construction of the single Comet 3 prototype, G-ANLO, was almost complete when the Comet 1 crash investigation began, meaning that it was too late to incorporate many of the major structural changes required, though fortuitously, the decision had already been made to incorporate oval cabin windows.

A certificate of airworthiness was issued for unpressurised flight, and flight testing began on July 19, 1954, with John Cunningham and Peter Buggé at the controls. Boeing's Model 369-80 had flown four days earlier.

Any hopes of a Comet 3 production programme were abandoned with the report into the Comet 1 crashes. The Comet 3 did not incorporate the fuselage-strengthening modifications required and incorporating them would have significantly delayed the Comet 3 test programme.

Instead, it was decided that the Series 3 Comet would not be put into production but would be succeeded by the Mark 4, which would embody the various improvements suggested by the enquiry. The sole Comet 3, G-ANLO, would be used as a development aircraft, primarily in support of the new Comet 4. A second Comet 3 airframe was not completed but was used for ground-based structural testing and the construction of another nine Comet 3 airframes was abandoned.

BELOW: The Comet 3 prototype was painted in a new BOAC colour scheme for its appearance at the 1957 Farnborough Airshow, with a dark blue tailfin. A similar scheme would subsequently be used by the production Comet 4s.

NAME CHANGER?

The new Comet Series 3 and Series 4 aircraft were so different to the previous variants that there was a suggestion that the name should be changed altogether. This suggestion was rejected by both de Havilland and BOAC, however, since both companies were keen to restore the Comet's reputation, and not to bury it!

Because the fuselage of the Comet 3 had not been modified as a result of Comet 1 accidents, it was not able to be fully pressurised, and the cabin was therefore pressurised to a differential of only 4lb per square inch, but this was sufficient for the aircraft's intended role, and meant that a cabin altitude of 10,000 ft could be maintained while flying at more than 20,000 ft.

Though structurally very different, the physical dimensions of the Comet 3 and the Comet 4 (which was officially announced in March 1955) were identical, apart from smaller nacelle tanks. This allowed the Comet 3 to be employed for Comet 4 development and especially for route-proving, and even for flying in support of eventual Comet 4 certification, which allowed service entry of the latter to be brought forward.

An aircraft that looked like the planned Comet 4 could thus be displayed at the 1954 and 1955 Farnborough Airshows, helping to build interest in the new type, and route proving flights included non-stop journeys to both Khartoum and Johannesburg – flights that previously required multiple fuel stops! These trips also allowed G-ANLO to record a number of speed records. On October 16, 1955, the aircraft flew from London to Khartoum at 523mph, while on October 23 and 24 its

flying time to Johannesburg was just 12 hours and 10 minutes – an average speed of 490mph.

WORLD TOUR

On December 2, 1955, John Cunningham, and Peter Buggé set off on a round-the-world demonstration flight, stopping at Cairo, Bombay, Singapore, and Darwin before a brief 'tour' of Australia and then flying home via Auckland, Fiji, Honolulu, Vancouver, Toronto, and Montreal. During the 26-day, 30,384 mile journey, 600 passengers experienced flying in the Comet, and a number of supernumerary crews from local airlines assisted on legs with which they were familiar. The aircraft was exposed to many different conditions on what were representative stages of a familiar trade route around the world, and data collected on the flights was found to be within very close tolerances of the flight planning data.

The Comet was designed to use airports and runways exactly as they were. When the aircraft arrived in Hawaii the observers from the Hawaiian Aeronautics Commission were amazed when the Comet landed on the short 7,000 ft runway and then pulled up within 3,000 ft to turn off at the intersection.

Trials of the Comet 3 in 1954 and 1955 meant that the brochure for the Comet 4 could be compiled in full confidence that its claims would be borne out in the production aircraft. That brochure was circulated to world airlines at the time of the SBAC Display in September 1955.

BOAC's order for 18 Comet 4 aircraft had been placed in March 1955, and the Comet 3's flight trials provided a useful indicator of what the production Comet 4 would be

capable of and provided welcome reassurance as to its likely operational performance.

In December 1956, G-ANLO was modified for further service, with engine bay modifications to allow the fitting of RA29 engines, and with detachable outer wing panels to allow the aircraft to be used to represent the new short haul Comet 4A.

In 1958 the aircraft was converted to Comet 3B configuration, to represent the Comet 4B that had been

ordered for BEA. This entailed the fitting of shortened outer wing panels, removal of the pinion tanks, and the fitting of a new storm warning radar and thrust reversers. The aircraft first flew in its new guise on August 21, 1958 and was demonstrated in BEA livery at the Farnborough Airshow in September 1958.

In June 1961, the aircraft was assigned to the Blind Landing Experimental Unit (BLEU) at RAE Bedford. In 1964, Hawker Siddeley used it to evaluate the Comet as a potential replacement for the RAF's Avro Shackletons. The Comet's low-speed handling was a distinct boon for the MPA role, and it was found that the aircraft could dash quickly to the target and then 'loiter' in the operational area.

The aircraft was damaged on April 19, 1971 during automatic landing system trials. While awaiting take-off clearance, XP915 was hit by a BEA Trident 3, G-AWZA. The impact caused compression damage to the fuselage and tore off the tailfin and part of the rudder.

The aircraft was repaired using the tailfin from a Comet C.Mk 2 ground instructional airframe at RAF Halton (XK716), which received a wooden tailfin in exchange. And XP915 was retired after making a final flight on April 4, 1972 and in 1973, the airframe was used for foam-arrester trials before the fuselage was sold to BAE Woodford, to serve as the mock-up for the Nimrod.

ABOVE: The Comet 3 was handed over to the Royal Aircraft Establishment at Bedford in 1961 and was assigned to the Blind Landing Experimental Unit. Fitted with a nose-mounted test instrumentation boom in 1966, the aircraft was then used for a variety of trials.

BELOW: After retirement from flying duties on April 4, 1972, the aircraft was used to assess a urea-formaldehyde foam arrester system intended to stop an aircraft in the event of a landing emergency.

de Havilland DH.106 Comet 3
Comet 3, G-ANLO, Ministry of Supply

c/n 06100, **Fate:** Became Comet 3B, XP915 with RAE. Retired in April 1972. Scrapped

The sole Comet 3 prototype in its original configuration, painted in BOAC colours. BOAC announced that it would place an order for five Comet 3s in December 1953, intending that the aircraft would form an 'express transatlantic fleet'. The Comet 3 prototype made its maiden flight in this guise (albeit without BOAC titles), on July 19, 1954, and flew in full BOAC markings at the 1955 Farnborough Airshow. It was also wearing this livery when it made a record-breaking round-the-world flight in December 1956. This was just one record set by G-ANLO, others including new speed records to Khartoum and Johannesburg.

The round-the-world flight included night stops, and local press and VIP flights were conducted along the route.

The Comet 3 was announced at the 1952 Farnborough Airshow, having been proposed by de Havilland as the next logical step in Comet evolution - an aircraft with longer range and a bigger payload. The new variant was given increased fuel capacity (8,308 imperial gallons) including new pinion tanks on the wing leading edge. The aircraft was powered by four new Avon RA16 engines rated at 9,000lb st, giving an estimated range of 2,700 miles or more, or 60% greater than the original Comet 1. The aircraft was able to cruise at Mach 0.74 with ease, and the aircraft was flown to a true Mach number of 0.81.

The fuselage was further stretched to 111' 6", allowing 58 passengers to be accommodated in an all first class configuration, or 76 tourist-class passengers.

Development of the Comet 3 continued even as the Comet 2 programme was abandoned, initially with the hope of attracting orders for the Comet 3 itself, and then in support of the planned Comet 4.

A number of airlines were interested in the Comet 3, including Pan American who wanted three (plus seven options) and who placed an order in October 1952, for delivery in 1956. Air India and KLM were also potential customers for the Comet 3.

BELOW: **The Comet 3 prototype under tow at Hatfield. British Aerospace announced the cessation of aircraft production at Hatfield from 1993 and the airfield closed In 1994, but the distinctive hangar and control tower was saved and is now a Grade II listed building, and home to a David Lloyd health club and gym!**

de Havilland DH.106 Comet 3B
Comet 3B, G-ANLO, Ministry of Supply

c/n 06100, **Fate:** Became XP915 with RAE. Retired in April 1972. Scrapped

G-ANLO, the sole completed Comet 3, was converted to Comet 3B standards in 1958, and was used to evaluate features of the Comet 4B that had been ordered by British European Airways (BEA). The wingspan was reduced by some seven feet, and wing leading edge pinion tanks were removed. Thrust reversers were fitted to the engines, and a storm warning radar was installed. The aircraft was also repainted in BEA's then current 'Peony' or triple crown livery and was flown during the 1958 SBAC airshow at Farnborough.

On December 1, 1958, the aircraft hit a tree on approach when the co-pilot accidentally selected 80° flap deflection instead of 60°, but the captain was able to recover and land safely, and the aircraft was repaired and was able to return to flight 15 days later.

Once Comet 4/4B testing was complete, the aircraft was used for investigating methods of preventing water ingestion when operating from wet runways. The aircraft made its last public appearance at the Hatfield Open Day in July 1960, before being handed over to the RAE at Bedford for experimental use, wearing RAF insignia, and the military registration XP915.

The aircraft was damaged on January 19, 1971, when it was hit by an over-shooting BEA Trident undertaking training at Thurleigh. The tail fin was torn off but was subsequently replaced by a tail taken from a redundant Comet 2.

The aircraft made its last flight on April 4, 1972, flying in formation with Comet 2E XN453 from Farnborough and the Bedford-based Comet 4 XV814 - the last occasion that a Comet 2, 3 and 4 would fly together.

After use for assessing a foam-based runway arrester system, the aircraft was broken up in 1973. The wings went to RAF Halton as a training aid and the aircraft's fuselage going to British Aerospace at Woodford to serve as a Nimrod MR.Mk 2 mock up (and then for Nimrod AEW.Mk 3 cabin layout tests) before being relegated to the fire dump in 1984.

BELOW: **The BEA colour scheme applied to G-ANLO featured an unusually high cheat line, leading forward from the tailplane to a point above the cockpit windows. Some believe that the Comet 3B, with its stretched fuselage and clean wing, was the nicest looking of all the Comet variants.**

The Pocket Rocket –
The Intercontinental Comet 4

The Comet 4 marked a triumphant return for the aircraft, its manufacturer and BOAC, beating the Boeing 707 across the Atlantic and kick-starting a new round of orders.

cycles (equivalent to 354,000 hours of flying) giving a safe life (with a scatter factor of six) of nearly 60,000 hours! But in a commendably thorough approach, de Havilland also ensured that if any cracks were to occur, then they would not propagate significantly for at least 6,000 flying hours, giving ample time for detection and rectification. Wing spars, lower wing skins and other potential areas of concern were similarly 'over engineered' and exhaustively assessed.

As a result of all this, no-one would ever call the Comet 4 'flimsy'!

And de Havilland went to just as much effort to ensure that their new Comet 4 would be as profitable as it was safe. Exhaustive market analysis indicated that only in the US domestic market, and perhaps on peak Atlantic routes, would an aircraft larger than their Comet 4 be needed. Everywhere else, the Comet was 'right-sized' and was optimised to return a healthy profit even when only half full! It was also pointed out that frequency of service was vital to passengers, making it advantageous to operate two services at the right time of day, rather than one flight by a bigger aircraft. And if traffic were to continue to increase at its then-current rate, de Havilland insisted, then the Comet 4 would remain 'right-sized' for the best part of the next eight to ten years on the Atlantic, and for the next ten to 15 years on other routes. This was, of course, for a Comet 4 that was nearly four years late – and what an on-time Comet 4 could

The Comet 1 disasters put paid to BOAC's original plan to operate a mixed fleet of Avon-engined Comet 2s and Comet 3s, but even by the beginning of 1955, the sole Comet 3 prototype was showing what an advanced, longer range Comet 4 might offer. And de Havilland was working out exactly how to build one!

Determined to avoid even the slightest concern about fatigue failures and explosive cabin decompressions, de Havilland set out to make the Comet 4's cabin 'unburstable', assessing the new structure to 118,000

LEFT: G-APDA is seen here under the floodlights at Heathrow. During early testing, the aircraft had a slightly different livery, with the cheatline terminating by wrapping round the windscreen. Subsequently, but before delivery to BOAC, the cheatline was extended down over the nose and 'chin'.

BELOW: Thanks to the work conducted by the Comet 3, G-ANLO, there was no need for a Comet 4 prototype, and the first aircraft built, G-APDA, went on to serve with BOAC after a short flight test programme, including hot and high trials at Khartoum, Nairobi, and Entebbe.

have achieved, beating the American Boeing 707 and DC-8 into service by several years, remains a fascinating 'what if'.

In February 1955, with such persuasive economic facts in front of him, BOAC chairman Sir Miles Thomas gave de Havilland an Instruction to Proceed with the manufacture of 19 'Intercontinental Comet 4s' for delivery between September 1958 and December 1959. This was even before the Comet 3 had made its round-the-world flight, and with the memory of the Comet 1 crashes still fresh in everyone's minds, it represented an extraordinary demonstration of faith in the aircraft, and in de Havilland.

It took until December 1956 for Thomas' successor, Basil Smallpeice, to negotiate a contract, and this was eventually signed on April 4, 1957. This laid down that the cost of each aircraft would be £1.16m (subject to inflation) and it was agreed that BOAC (named as a "most favoured customer") would receive the first four aircraft delivered to any airline and would get the same price if the aircraft was sold cheaper to any other party within two years of the delivery of its 19th aircraft. BOAC would be entitled to damages if the aircraft were not delivered within six months of the planned delivery date, and de Havilland was promised a bonus if it could give eight months' notice that the delivery of all 19 aircraft was being advanced. The contract also included the delivery of one Comet 2E.

By contrast, development of the aircraft itself was rapid and straightforward, and the first production aircraft, G-APDA, made its maiden flight on April 27, 1958. There was no prototype – but after the sterling work performed by the Comet 3, and by the two Comet 2Es (one owned by BOAC, the other by the Ministry of Supply), there was little need for one. It was once claimed that the Comet 4 had more than 50,000 hours of test and operational flying behind it – as well as a programme of scientific proving and ground testing that was unprecedented in aviation history. While G-APDA completed flight trials, G-APDB and G-APDC were officially accepted by BOAC on September 30, 1958. This was the date agreed in the contract, and all of the BOAC Comet 4 deliveries proceeded exactly according to plan with the 19th and last aircraft being delivered on January 11, 1960.

AMERICAN AMBITION

The next hurdle was to get the aircraft into service across the Atlantic, and this involved overcoming obstruction from the Port of New York Authority, which used allegations of excessive noise levels to try to block the Comet.

Eventually, on October 3, 1958, the Port of New York Authority authorised jet airliners to use the International

Airport at Idlewild. It stipulated many restrictions, but Comet performance was such that it was able to operate in and out of the airport with ease. G-APDC, captained by Roy Millichap, flew the first scheduled jet airliner service from London to New York the following day. Because of the prevailing winds the west-bound flight needed to refuel at Gander. A pre-positioned G-APDB flew a near-simultaneous and non-stop Eastbound service. In 1959 de Havilland, Rolls-Royce and BOAC were given the Hulton award for the most outstanding contribution to British prestige – for getting the Comet back into service.

The Comet had gone full circle. The aircraft had moved from triumph to tragedy before rising phoenix-like from the ashes of defeat. And in the process, the aircraft had been transformed from the 36-seat medium-range Comet 1 into the 81-seat transatlantic Comet 4, which was almost twice the size and had double the range of the Comet 1.

Pan Am began daily services to Paris with its Boeing 707s three weeks later, on October 26, 1958 and did so non-stop in both directions. But though the Boeing 707 was bigger and faster than the Comet, and did the journey non-stop in both directions, many passengers preferred to fly on the Comet, which was roomier, and which offered BOAC's legendary 'Monarch' cabin service. It felt more like luxury.

This was especially true on the two aircraft which opened the Comet 4's Atlantic service since they were configured as 48-seaters. The 16 deluxe seats in the forward cabin had a pitch of 56 inches, for which a

ABOVE: The first Comet 4 for Aerolineas Argentinas was named Las Tres Marias – the local name for the stars in 'Orion's belt'. The registration LV-PLM was replaced with LV-AHN on delivery. The delivery flight marked the first by a jet airliner between Europe and Latin America.

BELOW: John Cunningham tucks the gear up smartly as he takes LV-PLM aloft for an early test flight. The Comet 4 retained the delightful handling characteristics of earlier Comets but married these to a much stronger airframe and more powerful engines.

surcharge of £18 (almost double the average weekly wage) was payable. The 32 first class seats in the rear cabin were also luxurious by modern standards, at a round trip cost of £155!

And when a BOAC Comet captain spoke on the PA, he sounded confident and experienced on the route in a way that no Pan Am captain could. Pan Am 707 skippers were, after all, completely new to jets, where many of BOAC's captains had flown the Comet 1, and all had undergone a minimum of 50 hours of transatlantic and New York local route flying on the Comet 4, and many hours of Comet 2E flying - including eight transatlantic round trips totalling 120 hours.

Remarkably, there seems to have been no resistance to the Comet as a result of the fatal accidents four years earlier. Bookings for the Monarch service actually increased by 50% on the New York route after the Comet was introduced, and services were virtually sold out with load factors better than 80%. There was a particularly heavy demand for deluxe class seats, and this forced BOAC to modify the cabin layout of the Comet to increase their

number from 16 to 20. It should be noted that the Comet was priced at just over half of the cost of a Boeing 707.

The Comet 4s proved as popular with the engineers as they did with the accountants – displaying remarkably good serviceability. Weather delays were three times more common than technical, and there were only three unscheduled engine changes – and two of these were due to bird strikes!

BOEING CHALLENGE

But though the Comet 4 drove up traffic on the North Atlantic by a staggering 40%, BOAC opted to replace its Comet 4s on the North Atlantic run after two years of transatlantic operations. The Comet 4's replacements were the Conway-engined Boeing 707-436s that the corporation had ordered in 1956.

Before they left the North Atlantic, in October 1960, the BOAC Comet 4 fleet opened services to Canada with a once weekly flight from London to Montreal from December 1958.

BOAC had always intended to use its Comet 4s primarily on the old 'Empire' and Far East routes and had focused on

LEFT: Passengers disembark from East African Airways' inaugural Comet 4 jet service at Nairobi's Eastleigh Airport on September 18, 1960. A row of RAF Hawker Hunters shares the apron of what was then still RAF Eastleigh. Kenyan independence followed on December 12, 1963.

BELOW: BOAC's G-APDI was leased to AREA Ecuador from March 13, 1966 and served until impounded at Miami in March 1968. She was eventually cut up and scrapped in February 1978.

LEFT: **Dan-Air bought seven Comet 4s from BOAC as they were retired, and six more came from other airlines. With BEA Airtours Comet 4Bs and Dan-Air's Comets, Gatwick was briefly something of a Mecca for Comet enthusiasts.** (Chris England)

opening services to New York primarily to attract publicity, and to beat Pan Am and Boeing to the prize. North Atlantic Comet services had only ever been intended as a short term thing, and BOAC rapidly expanded its jet services on these routes, allowing the withdrawal of the Argonauts, Constellations and Stratocruisers, leaving the DC-7s, Britannias, and Comet 4s.

Services to South Africa resumed towards the end of 1959, followed by services to Tokyo, Hong Kong, Singapore, and Sydney. The Comet 4 was able to operate easily from runways that were too short for other jets. At Mauritius, for example, judged too short for a 707 by Air France, Comets were able to land and stop in just half the runway length.

In February 1959 captain Alabaster took the then Prime Minister, Sir Harold Macmillan, on a state visit to Russia in a Comet 4, for meetings with Nikita Khrushchev.

And BOAC Comet 4s continued to cross the South Atlantic. Rio de Janeiro's Galeão Airport had its runway extended to make it suitable for Comet 4 operations, allowing BOAC to include Rio on its scheduled London-Santiago service.

And though North Atlantic Comet services ceased in 1960, they resumed in September 1964, when Comet 4s were to be brought back on transatlantic routes to meet an unexpectedly heavy Scottish demand for flights! BOAC-Cunard operated three extra services a week during August and September. There would be a scheduled stopover at Gander, Newfoundland, and the return flight, from New York, would be made on the same day.

During 1964 BOAC let it be known that the time was approaching when it would start to dispose of some of its 19 Comet 4s and said that it expected two or possibly even three Comets to be surplus to its requirements during 1965. There had already been an enquiry from THY of Turkey who were considering taking one Comet 4 from BOAC, and the corporation began testing the second-hand market by offering one example for sale at an asking price of £600,000.

G-APDH was written off after a crash landing while on lease to Malaysian Airways in March 1964, but the remainder were sold off between December 1964 and January 1969. G-APDR was sold to Mexicana in December 1964, with G-APDT following in 1966.

BELOW: **Now an immaculately restored museum exhibit in full BOAC livery, G-APDB ended her working life, like so many Comets, with Dan-Air. Unlike most, she was not destined to be scrapped at Lasham, and is seen here making her last approach to Duxford's runway.** (Tony Clarke Collection via David Whitworth)

Malaysian Airways, previously a lessor of BOAC Comet 4s bought G-APDA, G-APDB, G-APDC, G-APDD and G-APDE during the second half of 1965, after which the Comet 4 was formally withdrawn from BOAC service. Captain Cliff Alabaster (who had flown the first Comet 1 commercial service 13 years earlier) commanded the final flight from New Zealand (via Australia and Singapore). This was made by G-APDM on November 24, 1965, after which he converted to the Vickers VC10.

G-APDI was leased to AREA Ecuador in May 1966, while G-APDG was sold to Kuwait Airways in December 1966. Two aircraft (G-APDF and G-APDS) went to the Royal Aircraft Establishment in March 1967 and January 1969 respectively, as XV814 and XW626, and the remaining seven were sold to Dan-Air between May 1966 and January 1969 (these were G-APDK, G-APDO, G-APDJ, G-APDN, G-APDL, G-APDM and G-APDP).

While BOAC sold the first of its outgoing Comet 4s for more than £600,000, it sold the remainder for a bargain basement £250,000 each. As a result, they sold like hot cakes! Thus ended BOAC's long association with the Comet – an aeroplane they had sponsored and supported from the beginning in 1946. BOAC had shown faith in the Comet 1 by placing advanced orders, and then showed faith in de Havilland by ordering the Mk.4 even after the

terrible accidents that had damaged its reputation along with that of the manufacturer.

But the Comet 4 probably marked the 'high water mark' of BOAC's relationship with the British aircraft industry, and thereafter, sometimes seemed to have its own agenda, which appeared to be to 'buy Boeing at all costs'. BOAC certainly chafed against the expectation that it would support the British aerospace industry. When it came time to replace the Comet 4, the carrier seemed set on 'rubbishing' the type, publicly explaining that with only 81 seats the Comets were not 'big enough', and inaccurately suggested that the type was 100 mph slower than the Boeing 707, and it initially had to be 'persuaded' to support the VC10.

OTHER OPERATORS

But BOAC was not the only operator of the Comet 4, even as a new-build aircraft.

Aerolineas Argentinas signed a contract for the supply of six Comet 4s worth more than £9m on March 19, 1958, and the Argentine government ratified the contract following the visit of an RAF Comet C.Mk 2 (and two Vulcan bombers) which participated in a flypast marking the inauguration of the new President, Arturo Frondizi. The Comet made a number of demonstration flights during the visit, and its ability to operate from short runways received favourable comment, as this was exactly why Aerolineas Argentinas had selected the aircraft.

De Havilland was able to divert the seventh, ninth and tenth Comet 4s from the BOAC order without interrupting its delivery schedule for the UK airline, and the first Aerolineas Argentinas Comet, LV-PLM, named *Las Tres Marias*, was delivered on March 2, 1959. The Argentinian Comets were configured with 24 first class seats forward and 43 tourist class seats aft, with an interior designed by Charles Butler Associates. Services to Santiago's Los Cerrillos began on March 28, and 'El Comet' flew a proving flight to New York's Idlewild on April 8, 1959.

The airline suffered several major accidents and purchased an additional Comet 4C in April 1962 to supplement

ABOVE: **After retirement from BOAC, and following leases to Air Ceylon, Kuwait Airways and MEA, the former G-APDS was sold to the MOD in 1969 for radar trials as XW626. She is seen here in 1977, shortly after the installation of a nose radome for the Marconi radar intended for the Nimrod AEW.Mk 3 programme.**

Kenya and Zanzibar (December 1963), and the subsequent merger of Tanganyika and Zanzibar (April 1964) with only the national flags on the tailfin changing to reflect the changed circumstances!

The first two Comets were withdrawn from use in November 1969 due to corrosion and were sold to Dan-Air for spares. The third followed in February 1971. Dan-Air in turn leased three Comet 4s to East African to 'plug the gap' in late 1970 and early 1971. These aircraft were G-APDD (5Y-AMT), G-APDE (5Y-ALF) and G-APDK (5Y-ALD).

Of the operators of ex-BOAC Comet 4s, AREA Ecuador withdrew its aircraft in March 1968, after two years' service, while Malaysian-Singapore Airlines sold its five aircraft to Dan-Air in 1969, one for spares use. Dan-Air also took Kuwait's sole Comet 4 in September 1969 and bought East African's three aircraft for spares use in 1970. Mexicana retired the last of its Comet 4s in 1979.

Dan-Air itself eventually had 19 Comet 4s, and flew 13 of them, some of them for only a single season. Dan-Air phased the type out after the 1973 season, and flew the last aircraft, G-APDB, to the museum at Duxford on February 12, 1974.

Dan-Air sold G-APDP to the RAE as XX944 in June 1973, but the aircraft was withdrawn from use in April 1975 after the discovery of severe corrosion. But two Comet 4s continued to fly as part of the MOD fleet. XW626 served as a radar testbed for the Nimrod AEW programme until it made its last flight on August 29, 1981. This left the RAE's XV814 as the last airworthy Comet 4. This navigation systems laboratory made its last flight on January 28, 1993, flying to Boscombe Down to serve as a spares source for the A&AEE's Comet 4C *Canopus*.

its remaining 4 Comets, which continued in use on international routes until they were gradually phased onto domestic routes between 1966 and 1968. They were finally sold to Dan-Air in 1971. One of the Aerolineas Argentinas aircraft (LV-AHU) enjoyed a brief flying career as G-AZIY, the others being broken up for spares.

The other purchaser of new Comet 4s was East African Airways, whose need for an aircraft that could operate from relatively short, hot-and-high runways made the type the obvious choice. East African Airways ordered a pair of Comet 4s (VP-KPJ and VP-KPK) in August 1958, and these were delivered in June and July 1960. The airline negotiated an agreement with BOAC to provide engine overhauls and to purchase engine hours from the British carrier when required.

VP-KPJ opened the London-Rome-Khartoum-Entebbe-Nairobi service on September 17, 1960. This was flown twice per week, with London- Rome-Khartoum-Nairobi-Dar-es-Salaam flown once per week. From January 1961, the EAA Comets began operating Nairobi-Karachi-Bombay services, and a third Comet (VP-KRL) was ordered for delivery in 1952.

The airline survived the granting of independence to Tanganyika (December 1961), Uganda (October 1962),

LEFT: **The last flying Comet 4 was XV814, a former BOAC aircraft sold to the MOD in 1967, and initially used as the trials aircraft for a new SIGINT collection system known as SLIS, housed in a capacious but detachable ventral bathtub. When this was not fitted a slimmer 'slipper pod' could be fitted, as seen here.**

de Havilland DH.106 Comet 4
Comet 4, G-APDR, BOAC

c/n 06418, **Fate:** Used for fire training after service with Mexicana. Scrapped

Initially registered as G-APDL, this BOAC Comet 4 was reallocated the registration G-APDR on the production line. She made her first flight on July 9, 1959 and was delivered to BOAC on July 20 the same year.

BOAC's Comet 4s wore a similar livery to the original Comet 1s, but with an all-blue tail fin, with the registration carried between two white stripes, below a larger Speedbird logo and a small Union flag.

The Comet 4 was designed for the Atlantic route, de Havilland taking the original Comet 1 and stretching it so that passenger capacity went from 36 to 81 and doubling the aircraft's range. At the same time, the aircraft was completely redesigned to solve the original Comet's fatigue issues. The result was the world's most advanced jetliner, though the larger Boeing 707 would soon eclipse the aircraft.

BOAC signed a contract to purchase 19 Comet 4s in April 1957 with the first two being delivered in September 1958 and the final one in January 1960. Initial deliveries of the BOAC Comet 4s were not fitted with Rolls-Royce thrust reversers, but G-APDR, the 14th aircraft, was the first Comet 4 to have them fitted as an optional extra.

Safe operation of the thrust reversers was demonstrated by Captain Perry on September 22, 1959 and following this demonstration it was deemed safe to have reverse thrust fitted on all the engines of the BOAC Comet 4 fleet.

During her time with BOAC, G-APDR was leased to Qantas (gaining 'QANTAS' titles above the cheatline) and to Malayan Airways.

G-APDR was sold to Mexicana on December 3, 1964 and was then registered as XA-NAZ and later as XA-NAP.

In June 1971, Channel Airways purchased the aircraft for her engines. She was flown to Stansted with almost 30,000 hours and after the removal of spares was donated to the CAA Fire Service at Stansted. Initially, the aircraft was used for non-destructive fire service training in the 1970s but was eventually used for actual fire training by the Stansted Fire Service, succumbing by 1981.

BELOW: **The smart BOAC Comet illustrated above went on to give seven years of service with Mexicana, before being purchased by Channel Airways for her engines. The redundant airframe ended her days with the Stansted Fire Service.**

de Havilland DH.106 Comet 4
Comet 4, LV-PLM, Aerolineas Argentinas

c/n 06408, **Fate:** Scrapped at Lasham

LV-PLM was the first Comet built for Aerolineas Argentinas. Its first flight was on January 27, 1959. The aircraft was handed over at a ceremony at Hatfield on February 27, 1959. Sir Aubrey Burke, managing director of de Havilland, unveiled the aircraft and presented it to Enrique Bermudez, technical director of Aerolineas Argentinas, the chairman of Aerolineas Argentinas and the Argentine ambassador.

John Cunningham was the pilot assigned to deliver LV-PLM to Argentina. The chairman of Aerolineas Argentinas had asked to arrive in Buenos Aires at exactly 4.00 pm. John Cunningham commented at the time that they didn't have a lot of experience flying to South America but deciding to leave after midnight and having time for a two hour break in Recife, he arrived at 4.00 pm as requested. He also set an unofficial record for the journey of 7,075 miles, taking 18 hours and 23 minutes.

At a ceremony attended by the President of Argentina and thousands of spectators, the president of Aerolineas Argentinas named the aircraft *Las Tres Marias*. With its delivery flight LV-PLM became the first jet airliner to travel from Europe to South America. It subsequently became the first jetliner to fly between North and South America.

In March 1959, this Comet was re-registered as LV-AHN and began commercial services flying from Buenos Aires to New York. The aircraft wore the normal Aerolineas Argentinas livery, with a blue cheatline and titles, and with the rudder 'striped' in the blue-white-blue of the national flag. The airline's condor logo was carried on the nose.

Aerolineas Argentinas received seven Comet 4s, but lost three in service, one during a training flight, and two in major fatal accidents. Despite this, the Comet brought a dramatic upward shift in passenger miles for the airline.

LV-AHN survived its time with Aerolineas Argentinas and was sold to Dan Air Services Ltd on December 4, 1971. The aircraft was scrapped at Lasham having flown 26,456 hours.

BELOW: Named *Las Tres Marías* on arrival in Argentina (the common local name for the three stars in the 'Belt of Orion'), this Comet was re-registered as LV-AHN in March 1959. The aircraft went on to be delivered to Dan-Air, who used her as a source of spares.

de Havilland DH.106 Comet 4
Comet 4, G-APDM, BOAC/QANTAS

c/n 06414, **Fate:** Scrapped at Lasham after subsequent service with MSA, MEA and Dan-Air

Qantas Empire Airways wet-leased six Comet 4 aircraft from BOAC between 1959 and 1963. These consisted of G-APDC, G-APDF, G-APDL, G-APDM, G-APDP, and G-APDR. The aircraft carried 'QANTAS' titles on the cabin roof in place of the standard BOAC titles, usually with the airline's winged Kangaroo logo on the tail fin, and often with 'repeater' 'QANTAS' titles on the pinion fuel tanks.

BOAC opened an inaugural London (Heathrow) - Sydney (Kingsford Smith) service on November 1, 1959, routeing London - Beirut - Karachi - Singapore - Sydney. But when Qantas inaugurated its own service with the leased Comets on November 7, it did so only on the London (Heathrow) - Singapore - London (Heathrow) sectors, routeing London - Athens - Teheran - Colombo - Kuala Lumpur - Singapore.

The chartered Comets allowed Qantas to add extra weekly services between Australia and the United Kingdom before they were returned to BOAC. G-APDM flew its final Qantas revenue service to Sydney (Kingsford Smith) airport on March 30, 1963 - two months before the final Qantas Comet 4 revenue service was flown from Singapore to London as QF745-053 on May 30, 1963.

Both Qantas and BOAC replaced the Comet 4 with the bigger, faster, and marginally more modern Boeing 707 on the London-Sydney route, but while the 707 did offer some advantages, it also necessitated a major runway lengthening at Sydney!

This aircraft operated its final BOAC Comet revenue service from Auckland to Heathrow on November 24, 1965 and was then leased to Middle East Airlines as OD-AEV from March 24, 1967, and to Malaysia Singapore Airlines from January 20, 1968 to September 6, 1968, using the registration 9V-BBJ.

G-APDM was returned to BOAC on the termination of the MSA lease and was then sold to Dan-Air (London) and registered to Dan-Air Services Ltd on September 4, 1969. The aircraft flew its last revenue service with Dan-Air on October 8, 1973.

After being withdrawn from use at Gatwick, the aircraft was used as a ground trainer, painted white overall and minus its outer wings.

BELOW: **BOAC's Comets enjoyed only a relatively short career with the airline before being sold on to other operators, but during that time, they found themselves leased to or chartered by a number of other airlines, giving many operators their first taste of jet operations.**

de Havilland DH.106 Comet 4
Comet 4, G-APDA, BOAC/Ghana Airlines

c/n 06401, **Fate:** Scrapped at Lasham

G-APDA was the first Comet 4 and was registered G-APDA on May 2, 1957. Chief test pilot John Cunningham, assisted by Pat Fillingham, E Brackstone-Brown, J Johnston, and J Marshall, made the first flight in the aircraft. It lasted one hour and 23 minutes and Cunningham reported that the Comet "behaved splendidly."

John Cunningham was at the controls for many of the aircraft's test flights. Over a period of 69 hours in 25 flights in July 1958 he evaluated the new Comet's performance, handling, auto-pilot, de-icing, and many other flight systems.

G-APDA was demonstrated at the Farnborough Airshow on September 5, 1958 and was subsequently flown to Hong Kong later that month to celebrate the opening of Kai Tak airport. The aircraft was the first to land and later to take-off from the new airport. Between September 16 and September 27, 1958 G-APDA was flown to Canada and then on to South America for sales demonstrations.

In March 1961 G-APDA was leased from BOAC for a short time to Ghana Airways, as shown here. Used as a VIP transport, the Comet was used to transport Ghana's first President, Kwame Nkrumah, to New York to attend a conference. The BOAC markings were replaced by those of Ghana Airways, although the basic BOAC colours remained the same. The Speedbird logos and the Union flag were removed from the tail and replaced by the Ghanaian flag above the registration on the tail. The Ghana Airways title and logo were placed above the cheat line with the Ghana Airways logo between the words 'GHANA' and 'AIRWAYS'. The aircraft was named *OSAGYEFO* (The Redeemer), and this was placed on the forward part of the aircraft behind the word 'COMET'.

In November 1969, at the end of its operational life, this Comet was sold to Dan Air Services. It was flown from Gatwick to Lasham and, having flown 29,416 hours, was used as a source of spares, and was then broken up in 1972.

BELOW: **This photo of G-APDA, the first Comet 4, shows her flying near Hatfield during an early test flight.**

de Havilland DH.106 Comet 4
Comet 4, G-APDF, BOAC/Malaysian Airways

c/n 06407, **Fate:** Became XV814, scrapped at Boscombe Down, 1997

During early service with BOAC, G-APDF was flown by the Shah of Iran in March 1959 and was used to prove the London-Tokyo route. Subsequently leased by Air Ceylon, the aircraft was later one of several leased by Malaysian Airlines for a 'Silver Kris Jet' service linking Singapore, Kuala Lumpur, Hong Kong, Jakarta, and Bangkok.

The first, G-APDH, was used from December 1962, when the airline was still known as Malayan Airways. The airline changed its name to Malaysian Airways after the 11 states of the Malayan Federation joined with Singapore, Sabah, and Sarawak to form the Federation of Malaysia.

BOAC Comets leased to Malaysian retained their BOAC tail markings, including both Speedbird and Union flag, but had 'MALAYSIAN AIRWAYS' titles above the cheatline, and the carrier's winged tiger's head logo on the forward fuselage. From September 1965, Malaysian began operating its own Comets (five aircraft purchased from BOAC), painted in its own markings, with a black and yellow cheatline and a yellow tail fin.

This Comet was sold to the MOD in January 1967 for use as a flying laboratory to replace Comet 2E XN453. As XV814, she was dispatched to Chester for modifications, emerging with a strengthened belly and provision for a slim 'slipper' pod, or a larger pod containing an experimental RAE SIGINT System known as SLIS (Side Looking Intercept System). In 1971, a Nimrod-type fin fillet was fitted to improve stability, then a wingtip pitot static system was added in 1972. 'Trials' work included some very 'operational' activities collecting IR signatures and data.

Painted in the MOD(PE) 'raspberry ripple' colour scheme in 1976, the aircraft served until December 18, 1992, when she was retired following a round-the-world trial from Farnborough. She was flown to Boscombe Down on January 28, 1993, to serve as a spares source for XS235 *Canopus*, and was put up for disposal in 1997.

BELOW: **After service with BOAC and MSA, G-APDF was sold to the MOD as a flying laboratory, to replace Comet 2E XN453. Serialled XV814, she carried a large equipment 'bathtub' under the nose – originally installed to accommodate the RAE's Side Looking Intercept System. She received a 'raspberry ripple' colour scheme in 1976.**

de Havilland DH.106 Comet 4
Comet 4, 5H-AAF, East African Airways

c/n 06443, **Fate:** Withdrawn in 1969 due to corrosion, scrapped at Lasham, 1973

This East African Airways Comet 4, 5H-AAF, is shown in the final colour scheme worn by the airline's Comets, after 1965, when the former British colonies of Kenya, Zanzibar, Tanganyika, and Uganda became independent. The original BOAC-like scheme, with EAA's winged lion emblem on the fin was replaced by a more colourful livery, with a striking green, yellow, red, and black colour scheme, with the flags of Tanzania, Uganda, and Kenya inside a sun logo on the tail fin, with the winged lion placed at the leading edge of the cheatline.

Originally registered as VP-KPK (a Kenyan registration), this Comet 4 first flew on July 28, 1960. She was handed over to East African Airways Corporation on September 6, 1960, the second aircraft to be delivered.

In January 1965, the airline's aircraft were re-registered to the respective countries, and each of the three Comets then in use was allocated to a different nation. VP-KPK was therefore re-registered 5H-AAF, reflecting notional Tanzanian ownership.

The East African Airways Corporation was an airline set up on January 1, 1946, headquartered in Nairobi, Kenya and jointly run by Kenya, Tanzania, and Uganda. The acquisition of the Comet allowed EAA to compete directly with BOAC

on its African routes and were instrumental in increasing the airline's profits from £40,000 in 1959 to £460,683 at the end of 1960. This led to an order for a third Comet at the end of 1960, delivered in April 1962. East African leased a further Comet 4 (G-APDL) from BOAC for an 18 month period from October 1965.

The Comets were finally withdrawn from scheduled services in November 1967. Thereafter, the aircraft were used by EAA's charter subsidiary, Seychelles-Kilimanjaro Air transport, though they retained EAA colours.

This Comet was withdrawn from use due to corrosion in November 1969, subsequently being sold to Dan-Air and flown to Lasham for spares recovery, before being scrapped in February 1973. The airline's Comet fleet staggered on, with the surviving aircraft augmented by one of three aircraft successively leased from Dan-Air.

BELOW: **The East African Airways Comet 4s initially wore a conservative livery, with a dark blue cheatline and the airline's winged lion badge in blue on the fin. The flags of Tanganyika, Zanzibar, Uganda, and Kenya were later added below the badge.** (Tony Clarke Collection via David Whitworth)

de Havilland DH.106 Comet 4
Comet 4, 9V-BAT, Malaysia-Singapore Airlines

c/n 06404, **Fate:** To Dan-Air in November 1970 and later scrapped

G-APDC was delivered to London Airport along with G-APDB and handed over to BOAC at an official ceremony on September 30, 1958. With the official US operating licence signed on the night of October 3, G-APDC was ready to make the first transatlantic jet flight.

Under the command of Captain Roy Millichap, the aircraft took off from London Airport at 9.55am on October 4 with a full complement of passengers and BOAC's chairman Sir Gerard d'Erlanger on board. The first transatlantic scheduled jet service took 10 hours and 22 minutes to reach New York. The British Prime Minister, Harold Macmillan, congratulated Sir Geoffrey de Havilland, saying: "a British aircraft has led the whole world into the new turbojet age."

In January 1959, the aircraft was used to conduct route-proving and check flights to Tokyo prior to the commencement of BOAC scheduled jet flights to the city. It returned to London on February 3.

On October 14, 1965 Malaysian Airways purchased G-APDC and it was re-registered 9M-AOC. However, after Singapore was granted independence in August 1965, Malaysian Airways became Malaysia-Singapore Airlines, and the aircraft was re-registered as

9V-BAT. Whilst being flown by Malaysian-Singapore Airlines the Comet was known as the Silver Kris Jet (the Kris is an asymmetrical dagger indigenous to Indonesia, Malaysia, Singapore, Thailand, and Brunei).

As 9M-AOC the aircraft displayed a yellow and dark blue cheat line with 'MALAYSIAN' above it and there were twin flags on the yellow tail. The colour scheme changed when Malaysian Airways became Malaysia-Singapore Airlines in 1966. The Malaysian and Singaporean flags were displayed on the nose below the cockpit and a stylised bird-like logo appeared on the tail fin.

On August 29, 1965 Malaysia-Singapore airlines sold the aircraft to Dan-Air Services Ltd for its charter flight business, although it didn't enter service for them until November 1970. Dan-Air finally retired this Comet on April 10, 1973 and it was flown to Lasham having accumulated 34,317 hours. This historic aircraft was sadly scrapped in 1975.

BELOW: **This MSA Comet 4, 9V-BAS, was the sistership of the aircraft illustrated above, but is also illustrated on page 53, when she was leased to Ghana Airways! She is seen here at a rainy Gatwick in 1969 – quite possibly immediately before her final flight to Lasham on November 19, 1969.** (Caz Caswell)

de Havilland DH.106 Comet 4
Comet 4, G-APDB, Dan-Air

c/n 06403, **Fate:** To Duxford in 1974

G-APDB is seen here in Dan-Air's original colour scheme, which was strongly reminiscent of the BOAC Comet 4 livery, with red largely replacing the blue, but with a largely white tail fin, and with red stripes above and below the registration.

This Dan-Air Comet 4 was one of five acquired from Malaysian Airways in late 1969. It had originally been delivered to BOAC in September 1958 as the Corporation's second Comet 4, until sold to Malaysian Airways as 9M-AOB in 1965 and delivered to its new operator on September 11, 1965. Malaysian became MSA (Malaysia-Singapore Airlines) in December 1966 and operated the five Comets until November 1969 when they were sold to Dan-Air.

Dan-Air was originally founded in 1953 as the airline subsidiary of shipbrokers Davies and Newman Holdings plc. The airline began scheduled services from Gatwick to Jersey in 1959, and soon decided to concentrate on inclusive tour (IT) and charter work, purchasing two ex-BOAC Mk.4s in May 1966. These were the first jets bought by a UK airline specifically for IT and charter work. Between 1967 and 1969 Dan-Air purchased five further Comet 4s from BOAC, and in late 1969, Dan-Air acquired five more ex-BOAC Comet 4s from Malaysia-Singapore Airlines - including G-APDB.

All the Mk.4s were converted to seat 99 passengers and were later reconfigured to seat 106. This required the cabin floor to be strengthened, while the wing structure was stiffened to withstand the stresses imposed by more frequent landings.

G-APDB flew the last Comet 4 commercial service on November 13, 1973, and was then retired to the IWM at Duxford, on February 12, 1974, becoming the first aircraft in what became the British Airliner Collection.

In BOAC service G-APDB had made aviation history on October 4 when it operated the first scheduled service by a jet powered airliner from New York to London, in the then record time of 6 hours 11 minutes. This was reflected in 2007, when the aircraft was restored and repainted in BOAC markings.

BELOW: **This pair of Dan-Air Comet 4s, seen at Gatwick in 1967, were sisters of the aircraft illustrated above, and show to advantage variations in the early Dan-Air livery, with each aircraft having its registration applied in a different colour, and with slight variations in the airline titles.** (Caz Caswell)

Short-haul –
The Gentle Jet

De Havilland wanted a short-haul 'regional jet' as well as an aircraft with intercontinental range. After something of a false start with the Comet 4A, the further stretched Comet 4B fitted the bill very nicely indeed!

ABOVE: Named *Walter Gale*, G-APMB flew BEA's first jet service, which was from Tel Aviv to London on April 1, 1960. Her flying career lasted until December 28, 1978, when she made her final flight in Dan-Air service. Subsequently the aircraft was used (minus her outer wings) for training tug drivers at Gatwick airport.

While the Intercontinental Comet 4 was under development, de Havilland started to consider a number of Comet 4 sub-variants. The first of these was the Comet 4A, which was launched in June 1956 as a short range version of the Comet. It was described as a 'Short to Medium-haul, Express Airliner' and as offering airlines a high-speed jet aircraft that would be capable of operating over short and medium stage routes at a competitive cost.

The Comet's relatively short take-off and landing performance meant that it was well suited to operating from regional airports, which might have shorter runways than the major hubs. This made the Comet a regional jet before such a term had been coined!

The all-up weight of the new Comet 4A was planned to be the same as for the Comet 4 (e.g., 152,000lb), but the new version incorporated a 40in fuselage stretch and effectively sacrificed fuel capacity for more seats. This allowed up to 70 passengers to be carried in a four abreast, all-first class layout, or up to 92 passengers in a higher density, five abreast tourist class configuration. A range of alternative seating options were of course possible.

The wingspan of the Comet 4A was reduced from 115ft to 108ft to reduce drag at lower altitudes. This change, along with some structural strengthening of the rear fuselage and tail, and the introduction of new operating procedures, enabled the Comet 4A to operate at higher cruising speeds. By flying at lower altitudes, the Comet 4A's true airspeed was increased relative to the limiting

Mach number. As a result, the Comet 4A was able to cruise at between 520 and 545mph at 23,500ft (the differences being due to variations in the ambient air temperature). Though the Avon engines burned more fuel at this lower cruising altitude, this was more than offset by the increase in cruising speed and shorter journey times.

It was calculated that the Comet 4A would offer good operating economy on stage lengths of between 500 miles and 2,000 miles. Above this distance higher altitudes were recommended. But with its maximum payload of 22,690lb (92 passengers) the Comet 4A's maximum stage length in still air was quoted as 1,880 miles (with full fuel reserves). The maximum stage length figure increased to 2,040 miles when carrying a 19,070lb payload (e.g., in the 70 seat, all first class configuration).

The new version seemed particularly well optimised for internal American routes, and soon attracted the interest of Capital Airlines, who had identified the need for a higher capacity aircraft.

Capital Airlines placed a substantial £19m order for four Comet 4s and ten Comet 4As in August 1956 and planned to operate the Comet 4A on the New York – Chicago route from January 1, 1959. It was calculated that, as a result of the Capital contract, de Havilland would require another 800 staff.

De Havilland could be confident that the Comet 4A would be delivered quickly, and 'on spec', as the configuration could be proven on the sole Comet 3, which, from January 1957, used the same type of Avon engines and was fitted with detachable outer wings to allow the 4A outer wing to be installed. This effectively meant that a fully representative prototype would be flying 18 months before the first Comet 4A was completed and would have been available for much of the required certification flying.

Unfortunately, no Comet 4As were built as the launch customer, Capital Airlines, cancelled the order. Capital had got into short term financial difficulties and by the time these were resolved the airline had been absorbed by United Airlines. United had originally been formed from Boeing's own commercial airline and as such was unlikely to want to honour Capital's Comet purchase!

But, while the Comet 4A didn't happen, it laid the groundwork for another short-haul variant, the Comet 4B.

This new variant was developed for BEA as something of a stop gap. Air France's order for the Caravelle twin-jet made BEA's propeller-driven Vickers Viscounts look decidedly old-fashioned, and the proposed DH121 Trident would not be in service until 1964. The Comet promised to give BEA a short-haul jet quickly, and in 1957 the airline placed an order for six, eventually taking 14 by exercising all of its options. Four more were acquired by Olympic Airways who would operate the type in co-operation with the BEA Comet fleet. Although originally purchased as a stop-gap, the Comet

ABOVE LEFT: **This Comet 4B, G-APMF, named 'William Finlay', flew the first BEA jet service to Moscow on April 1, 1960. The aircraft is seen here after its arrival in Moscow, with Lord Douglas of Kirtleside, BEA's chairman, among the 81 passengers.**

ABOVE RIGHT: **Taxiing past propeller-driven BEA and Lufthansa Vickers Viscounts at London's Heathrow Airport, BEA's Comet 4B G-APMC (*Andrew Crommelin*) looks the epitome of modernity, with its funky 'Red Square' livery, swept wing, and jet engines. Andrew Claude de la Cherois Crommelin (to give him his full name) was an English astronomer of French and Huguenot descent who had died in 1939. Only the first nine Comet 4Bs were named.**

LEFT: **The BEA 'Flying Jack' livery, (retrospectively more widely known as 'Speedjack' or 'Quarterjack'), was designed by Henrion design Associates and was introduced from late 1968. It is seen here on G-APMD, *William Denning*, named after another British astronomer.**
(Malcolm Nason)

The Comet 4B was the fastest of the breed, proving capable of cruising at up to 532mph, with an optimum cruising speed of 520mph at 23,500ft. At a weight of 135,000lb this gave a fuel consumption of 11,500lb/hr. Fuel capacity was reduced to 7,890 imperial gallons, but the aircraft could still carry 84 passengers over stages of more than 2,000 miles.

BEA's first two Comet 4B aircraft (G-APMB and G-APMC) were handed over at Heathrow on November 16, 1959 – ten weeks ahead of schedule. A dispute with pilots over pay and working conditions delayed service entry until April 1, 1960, when G-APMB flew from Tel Aviv-Athens-Rome-London, with other Comet 4Bs inaugurating the London-Moscow, Moscow-London, and London-Nice services on the same day.

The Comet 4B had a relatively short career with BEA, but a busy one. Mediterranean destinations were also served by Olympic's Comet 4Bs and by BEA Comets operating under a Cyprus Airways flight number.

Two aircraft were lost in service. G-ARJM stalled on take-off at Ankara on December 21, 1961, killing the crew of seven and 20 passengers, though seven passengers were thrown clear and survived.

The second aircraft to be lost was G-ARCO, which was destroyed by a terrorist bomb on October 12, 1967. The aircraft crashed into the Mediterranean near Rhodes, killing all 66 on board. Coincidentally, both aircraft were operating under Cyprus Airways flight numbers when they were lost.

Though BEA flew its last scheduled Comet 4B service in June 1969, two Comet 4Bs (G-APMA and G-APME) continued to operate, having been retained to fill gaps caused by the late delivery of Trident 3s, and three Airtours aircraft were subsequently leased back to BEA for the same purpose. G-APMA finally flew the last BEA Comet 4B service from Malaga to London on October 31, 1971.

Initially seven (and eventually ten) of the BEA aircraft were allocated to BEA Airtours, the new wholly-owned, Gatwick-based IT charter division that had been established in March 1969. Operating in a 109 seat all tourist configuration, G-ARJL flew the first service to Palma on March 6, 1970.

But the BEA Comet operation was a victim of its own success, with a huge growth in passenger numbers meaning that Airtours soon needed a larger aircraft. BEA sought permission to buy seven ex-American Airlines Boeing 707-123Bs, but this was not granted, and instead, ex-BOAC 707-436s were delivered from December 30, 1971.

4B proved to be ideally suited to BEA's short-haul European routes, and as the certificated weight of the 4B increased so too did its range and eventually it was used on longer routes.

The Comet 4B combined the longer fuselage of the proposed intercontinental Comet 4C with the shorter wings of the Comet 4A. This represented a further 38in fuselage stretch compared to the 4A, making the new variant 6ft 6in longer than the Comet 4, with a fuselage length of 118ft.

The wing span was reduced to 107ft 6in, with a corresponding reduction in wing area to 2,059ft^2. No pinion tanks were fitted. Removal of these tanks was found to induce a heavy pre-stall buffet, and to cure this, spoilers were fitted to the leading edge and the wing fence was moved inboard by about four feet. The fence had previously concealed some wiring, which was now covered by a conduit. Once modified, the Comet displayed viceless handling characteristics, prompting BEA's Comet flight manager, captain Geoff Greenhalgh to call it 'the gentle jet'.

Maximum take-off weight was initially set at 158,000lb (though this was increased in stages to 162,000lb) with a capacity payload of 24,137lb. With its increased all up weight and stretched fuselage, the Comet 4B could accommodate from 84 to 102 seats – three times more than the original Comet 1!

ABOVE: **Seen here on a pre-delivery test flight, G-APYC became SX-DAK with Olympic Airways, with whom she was named 'Queen Frederica'. The aircraft wears the original Olympic livery, with a rectangular Greek flag on the forward fuselage.**

BELOW: **The same aircraft, SX-DAK, is seen here in Olympic's later livery, with a wavy triangular flag, and 'Airways' dropped from the airline's title, which is applied in a bolder typeface.** (Malcolm Nason)

RIGHT: Olympic's SX-DAO (*Queen Sophia*) is seen refuelling at Gibraltar. The aircraft served with Olympic from March 1963 until April 1969, initially registered as G-ARDI. She later served with Channel Airways, and ended her days scrapped at Southend airport.

BELOW: This Comet 4B, G-APMG, began life as *John Grigg* with BEA, before going on to BEA Airtours and Dan-Air. She is seen here in Dan-Air's second livery, with a red tailfin and a black 'underline' below the cheatline. She served with Dan-Air until November 1977. (Rob Hodgkins)

The ten Comet 4Bs were sold to Dan-Air. Two were sold in 1972, and three more in January and February 1973. The final five followed after the 1973 summer season. The final Airtours Comet service was flown by G-ARJL on October 31, 1973, and the aircraft made the last flight in BEA markings on November 9, 1973.

The other mainline carrier to operate the Comet 4B was Olympic Airways. Olympic owner Aristotle Onassis and Lord Douglas of Kirtleside, BEA chairman, signed an innovative consortium agreement that brought the Greek airline into the jet age, operating its Comets in co-operation with BEA. This arrangement effectively treated the aircraft as a single fleet, and on occasion an Olympic crew would fly a BEA Comet, and vice versa. Interestingly, Olympic chose to operate their aircraft with two pilots and a flight engineer, whereas BEA had three pilots on the flight deck.

Initially, Olympic bought two Comet 4B aircraft. SX-DAK, named *Queen Frederica*, was handed over on April 26, 1960, and SX-DAL (*Queen Olga*) followed on May 14, 1960. Subsequently, two more aircraft were leased from BEA. G-APZM (*Queen Sophia*) was initially leased from July 1960 to April 1966, before becoming SX-DAN.

G-ARDI (*Princess Sophia*) was leased from March 1961, later becoming SX-DAO.

The leased aircraft were returned to BEA in 1969 and 1970, and title in the other two was transferred to BEA to allow them to be disposed of as a single fleet.

In the event, the four former Olympic Comet 4Bs were sold to Channel Airways, together with one BEA aircraft (G-ARDI). They arrived at Stansted between January and June 1970 after storage at Cambridge, and were quickly pressed into service, operating flights from Birmingham, Bristol, East Midlands, Glasgow, Manchester, Newcastle, and Stansted. The ex-BEA aircraft was retired in June 1971, and the rest followed a few months later, when Channel Airways went into receivership on February 1, 1972. Its Comets were sold to Dan-Air.

Dan-Air eventually acquired 15 Comet 4Bs, 12 of which were put into service, with three being stripped for spares. These were operated in a very high density 119-seat layout. Seven of the final eight Comet 4Bs were retired after the 1978 season, and the last Comet 4B service was flown by G-APYD on October 23, 1979, before the aircraft was retired to the Science Museum at Wroughton.

de Havilland DH.106 Comet 4B
Comet 4B, G-ARGM, BEA

c/n 06453, **Fate:** Scrapped at Lasham, April 1975

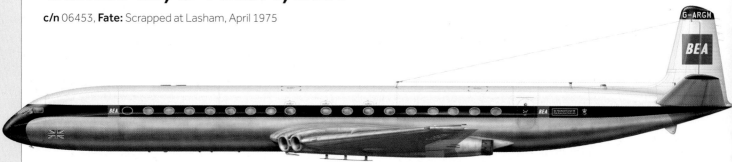

BEA's G-ARGM was originally built as G-AREI, but this registration was not taken up. She was unnamed. She is shown here in BEA's striking and iconic 'Red Square' livery - the logo reportedly drawn up by Mary de Saulles, the airline's industrial designer on her dining table over supper.

The introduction of the new tail badge was accompanied by a new colour scheme with a plain black cheatline extending forward to a black nose and cockpit framing, and with bright red wings (apart from the leading edges and trailing edge control surfaces) - allegedly to make them highly visible following a series of collisions. The black cheatline initially divided the white top from polished natural metal or silver-painted undersides, before a switch to light grey under surfaces.

A larger version of the 'Red Square' logo was applied from about 1960, and this scheme became almost synonymous with the 'Swinging Sixties' - bold, brash, funky, and modern. It was, however, relatively short-lived, with a new 'Flying Jack' colour scheme coming into use from 1968.

G-ARGM made her first flight on April 27, 1961 and she was delivered to BEA on May 6, 1961. BEA's fleet, including G-ARGM, gave excellent service throughout the sixties. Sister aircraft G-ARJM was lost in a take-off accident at Ankara in December 1961, killing all but seven of the 34 on board,

and briefly raising the spectre of the earlier Comet disasters, but confidence in the aircraft was not dented. Many new destinations were added to the Comet schedule by the summer of 1963.

G-ARGM was withdrawn from BEA services in the autumn of 1969 and was transferred to BEA Airtours Ltd in March 1970, and then sold to Dan-Air Services Ltd in November 1973.

G-ARGM's final flight proved to be the delivery from Gatwick to Lasham, ending 24,405 flying hours and 14,196 flights. She never entered service with Dan-Air, never flew again and was broken up for spares at Lasham in April 1975.

RIGHT AND BELOW: After service with BEA Airtours, this Comet 4B, G-ARGM, ended her days being stripped for spares and then scrapped at Lasham in April 1975. This was probably the most common end for the Comet 4s, 4Bs and 4Cs!

de Havilland DH.106 Comet 4B
Comet 4B, SX-DAO, Olympic Airways

c/n 06447, **Fate:** Scrapped at Southend, 1972

This Comet 4B began and ended its working life as G-ARDI, but is seen here as SX-DAO, wearing the livery of Olympic Airways, including the unusual rear fuselage marking that extended down from the cheatline that was seen on some Olympic and Channel Airways Comet 4Bs. The basic scheme was otherwise very similar to that applied to BOAC's Comet 4Bs, albeit with Olympic titles and the airline's 'Olympic Rings' logo. Olympic Airways named the aircraft *Princess Sophia*.

Aristotle Onassis' Olympic Airways and BEA had formed the 'Anglo-Greek Consortium' to operate two newly purchased Comet 4Bs, and two leased from the UK carrier - these latter aircraft were additional to BEA's original 14 aircraft.

The Olympic-owned aircraft were SX-DAK (G-APYC) *Queen Frederica* and SX-DAL *Queen Olga* (G-APYD) while the BEA aircraft were G-APZM (later SX-DAN) *Queen Sophia* and G-ARDI (later SX-DAO) *Princess Sophia*. The BEA and Olympic Comets were used on routes out of Athens to Amsterdam, London, Brussels, Rome, Paris, Frankfurt, Zurich, Istanbul, Cairo, Beirut, and Tel Aviv.

G-ARDI first flew on March 18, 1961 and was purchased by BEA for long-term lease to Olympic. The aircraft was

re-registered as SX-DAO in 1966 and served Olympic Airways until 1969.

When the aircraft was withdrawn from service, she was flown to Cambridge Airport for storage pending her sale along with the rest of the Olympic Comet fleet.

On November 5, 1969, SX-DAO was assigned back to BEA and was transferred from Cambridge to London Airport. In April the following year she was sold to Channel Airways, flying again as G-ARDI. She flew to Channel Airways' base at Stansted and served the company for around 18 months. G-ARDI was flown to Southend for scrapping in October 1971 having completed 11,960 flights, amassing 20,148 hours.

After the collapse of Channel Airways in 1972, all of their Comets became available for purchase. Dan-Air acquired G-ARDI for possible spares recovery at Lasham, but it was instead scrapped at Southend two months later.

BELOW: **Olympic Airways was established by the Greek shipping magnate, Aristotle Socrates Onassis, who had already amassed the world's largest privately-owned shipping fleet. On being told that he could not use the five Olympic rings as the airline's logo due to copyright issues, he simply decided to add a sixth ring!**

de Havilland DH.106 Comet 4B
Comet 4B, G-APMF, BEA

c/n 06426, **Fate:** Scrapped at Lasham c.1974 after serving with BEA Airtours and Dan-Air

G-APMF was the fourth of BEA's ten Continental Comet 4Bs, named as *RMA William Finlay*, and delivered to BEA at London Airport on January 27, 1960, having made her first flight on January 5, 1960. She is seen here in BEA's distinctive later 'Flying Jack' or 'Speed Jack' livery designed by Henrion Design Associates. The new colour scheme was based on a 'Cosmic Blue' cheatline and tail, with a new tail badge that was intended to symbolise Britain and flying - with the Union jack 'arrowhead' supposedly representing an aeroplane. With the large Union jack-based tail badge taking such prominence, the smaller traditional representations of the British national flag that had been applied since 1950 disappeared. Red wings were retained (largely on cost grounds), but the new blue cheatline did not extend over the nose. A new, more angular BEA logo was designed, and new cabin crew uniforms were designed by Hardy Amies, including a bright red overcoat for stewardesses. The re-branding cost a reported £100,000 and individual aircraft were repainted as they went in for a major overhaul.

BEA initially ordered six 100-seat short-to-medium range Comet 4Bs for their short-haul business in August 1957. The cost was £7m. Deliveries were to begin late in 1959 and to be completed by the spring of 1960. However, on June 24, 1960

BEA increased its order to 10 Comet 4Bs, including this aircraft, G-ARGM, and the airline eventually received all 18 of the type. One BEA Comet 4B, G-ARCO, disappeared during a flight from Athens to Nicosia, the cause subsequently being found to be a terrorist bomb. All 59 passengers and seven crew perished.

G-APMF was transferred to BEA Airtours in April 1970, serving BEA's charter operation for two and a half years. On 31 January, 1973 it was retired from BEA Airtours and sold the same day to Dan-Air.

It flew for Dan-Air for almost two years, but was withdrawn from service on November 5, 1974, making its last flight to Lasham having clocked up 29,587 flying hours and 17,412 flights.

RIGHT AND BELOW: The Airtours variant of the Flying Jack livery is seen here on G-ARGM (right) and on a sister aircraft of the profile subject, G-ARJK. The livery was designed by Henrion Design Associates using a 'cosmic blue' colour that could appear very dark under some lighting conditions. (Chris England and Norbert Kripfl)

de Havilland DH.106 Comet 4B
Comet 4B, G-ARJL, BEA/Olympic

c/n 06455, **Fate:** Scrapped at Lasham

This Comet 4B (also illustrated on page 67) was leased to Olympic Airways from February 1964 until February 1970, and during that period flew with a number of variations to its basic Olympic Airways livery, but never with a Greek registration!

In August 1964, the aircraft was seen with a Cyprus Airways logo aft of the rear passenger door, and soon afterwards was spotted with a BEA Red Square logo aft of the rear passenger door. These were temporary stickers, and Olympic and Cyprus Airways logos were sometimes also attached to BEA Comet 4Bs when they operated services for these airlines.

By January 1969 she carried the later Olympic scheme, with bold titles and a 'wavy' Greek flag. A Red Square logo was superimposed on the cheatline just aft of the forward passenger door, level with the flag, on the starboard side.

By April 1969, all Olympic titles and badges had disappeared altogether, and the aircraft carried a large Red Square badge on the tail, with smaller logos on the cheatline, fore and aft.

G-ARJL was the 12th BEA Comet 4B, delivered to the airline on May 31, 1960. She flew her first service to Tel Aviv on June 4, 1961. On departing from Nicosia, the aircraft experienced undercarriage retraction problems and had to dump fuel and return to Cyprus to land. BEA reported at least 13 defects on the flight. Later in her career, the aircraft suffered a fire in the rear luggage bay but was able to land safely.

She was later passed to BEA Airtours and had the distinction of making the first and last Airtours flights. The first, on March 6, 1970, was to Palma, and the last, on October 31 was a National Union of Students charter from Paris to Gatwick.

The aircraft was subsequently sold to Dan-Air but was broken up for spares without entering Dan-Air service, ending her days, like so many of the breed, at Lasham.

BELOW: **This sister aircraft to the profile subject looks remarkably similar. BEA acquired the title to G-APYC on August 14, 1969, and quickly stripped off Olympic Airways titles and logos. BEA logos were not applied in this case, and the aircraft was sold to Channel Airways.** (Chris England)

de Havilland DH.106 Comet 4B
Comet 4B, G-ARDI, BEA

c/n 06447, **Fate:** Scrapped at Southend

Channel Airways won a major new contract in April 1969 to provide services during the 1970-72 holiday seasons, and this required the Stanstead based carrier to acquire additional aircraft. Channel therefore purchased an ex-BEA Comet 4B aircraft and four stored ex-Olympic Airways Comet 4Bs at a cost of just under £2m. They were sold to Channel Airways on April 17, 1970 and flown to Stansted. One of the latter was G-ARDI, seen here. The five Comets were fitted out in a 106-seat configuration suited to the airline's holiday charter work.

Olympic Airways had withdrawn G-ARDI (then flying under the registration SX-DAO) from service in 1969. By then she had amassed 17,569 flying hours and completed 10,570 flights.

Most of the Channel Airways fleet wore an attractive colour scheme, with a black and gold tail fin, a gold twin cheatline above the cabin windows, and a red pinstripe below them, dividing the white fuselage top from the grey undersides. The Comets, by contrast, retained the basic colours of their original owners. The BEA aircraft simply had its Red Square logos overpainted, and even retained red painted wings! The ex-Olympic airlines had their tail fin logos overpainted in a

nearly-matching blue, and all received 'CHANNEL AIRWAYS' titles. None received the full Channel Airways livery.

During the 1970 holiday season, Channel Airways Comets were flown from Birmingham, East Midlands, Bristol, Manchester, Glasgow, Newcastle, and Stansted. Channel had planned to phase out the Comets after the 1972 season and for that third season of the contract the aircraft were to have operated under Air England branding. The original contract, however, was not renewed and no Comets ever carried the Air England livery.

G-ARDI was withdrawn from service in September 1971, and on October 21 was flown to Southend for scrapping. By then she had amassed a total of 20,148 flying hours and had completed 11,960 flights.

Channel ran into financial difficulties in 1972 and the airline passed into the hands of the receiver. The surviving Comets passed to Dan-Air.

BELOW: **Channel Airways' fleet of five Comet 4Bs retained their original basic colours whilst in service with the charter airline – and in four cases this meant the Olympic Airways scheme. They were primarily used to operate IT charters for the Lyons Tours Travel Agency, operating in a 109 seat configuration.** (Tony Clarke Collection via David Whitworth)

de Havilland DH.106 Comet 4B
Comet 4B, G-ARJL, BEA Airtours

c/n 06455, **Fate:** Scrapped at Lasham c.1974

After their withdrawal from BEA scheduled services in March 1969, several Comet 4Bs were retained to cover for delays to Trident deliveries, and indeed unserviceability. Ten aircraft were withdrawn from storage at Cambridge to form the initial core of the newly formed BEA Airtours charter business. BEA had launched a tour operator subsidiary, Silver Wing Holidays, in April 1964, and BEA Airtours formed as a dedicated charter division on April 24, 1969. Airtours initially operated Comets that had been retired from mainline operations, adding a 'BEA Airtours' logo above the cheatline, but otherwise retaining the airline's 'Flying Jack' livery.

G-ARJL first flew on May 19, 1961 and was delivered on May 31. She was the 12th BEA Comet 4B, part of a final batch of four aircraft and entered service on June 4, 1961. The aircraft was leased to Olympic Airways in February 1964 and after six years of service returned to BEA in February 1970. A month later she was transferred to BEA Airtours Ltd.

Her first flight for Airtours on March 6, 1970 was actually the company's very first charter. Flight KT243 took off that afternoon from Gatwick, bound for Majorca's Palma airport.

She was crewed by captain Peter McKeown, first officer Peter Jarvis and first officer Geoffrey Evans.

The Comet was a victim of its own success with BEA Airtours, with rapid success generating an urgent need for a larger and more capacious replacement, which was found in the shape of ex-BOAC Boeing 707s.

G-ARJL's last commercial flight was the last Airtours Comet service - a charter flight for the National Union of Students from Paris Le Bourget to Gatwick on October 31, 1973.

Dan-Air purchased G-ARJL on November 8, 1973, along with her nine Airtours sisters, and she was flown from Gatwick to Lasham where four of the ten aircraft were to be used for spares, including 'Juliet Lima'. After touching down at Lasham, the aircraft had completed 15,006 flights and had flown a total of 25,379 hours.

BELOW: **The starboard side of the aircraft illustrated above! Judging by the youth of the disembarking passengers and their hairstyles and clothing, this is probably the aircraft's final flight – a charter from Le Bourget to Gatwick for the National Union of Students.**

de Havilland DH.106 Comet 4B
Comet 4B, G-APMB, Dan-Air

c/n 06422, **Fate:** Sold to Gatwick Handling for training use in 1978, scrapped at Gatwick c.2003

This Comet 4B was acquired from Channel Airways in 1972 with three of her sisters, joining the Lasham-based airline's first two Comet 4Bs. Dan-Air eventually received 15 Comet 4Bs, though four of these never entered service, and were stripped for spares and scrapped.

G-APMB originally served with BEA, named *RMA Walter Gale*. She joined the airline in November 1959, after starring at the 1959 Farnborough Airshow. She then gained a measure of fame by flying BEA's first jet service on April 1, 1960.

After a brief lease to Olympic Airways, 'Mike Bravo' was sold to Channel Airways in June 1970, retaining her basic BEA livery with 'CHANNEL AIRWAYS' above the cheatline and a plain white tail fin. The addition of five Comet 4Bs marked a major expansion of Channel's jet operation, turning the carrier into a leading UK charter airline. IT operations accounted for more than half of its business, but the seasonal peaks and troughs in the charter and scheduled markets drove up Channel's unit costs and led to financial difficulties. This aircraft was withdrawn from service in January 1972, with the collapse of Channel Airways. She was ferried to Lasham on April 9, 1972, joining Dan-Air.

In Dan-Air service, the longer fuselage Comet 4Bs were re-fitted for 119 seats. Flight Services lightweight seats were used to keep the additional weight down.

G-APMB made her last flight on December 28, 1978 and was sold to Gatwick Handling for training use. Painted white and stripped of her interior, the aircraft was used for training ground handlers in aircraft towing. She was finally unceremoniously scrapped in July 2003. By then she had outlived Dan-Air. The airline went into decline, and it failed to 'vertically integrate' with an IT operator, while the airline's inefficient fleet mix made Dan-Air uncompetitive, making its end inevitable. It began making losses from 1989, and, following unsuccessful attempts to merge Dan-Air with a competitor, the ailing airline was sold to British Airways in 1992 for the nominal sum of £1.

BELOW: **This is the same aircraft as is shown in the illustration above, but in Dan-Air's later red-tailed livery. After service with BEA and Channel Airways, the former** *Walter Gale* **went on to fly seven seasons with Dan-Air, ending in December 1978.** (Caz Caswell)

de Havilland DH.106 Comet 4B
Comet 4B, G-APMG, Dan-Air

c/n 06442, **Fate:** Scrapped at Lasham c.1978

This Comet 4B made its maiden flight on July 25, 1960 and was delivered to BEA as *RMA John Greig* on July 31. After ten years, the aircraft was transferred to BEA Airtours who used her until October 1973, when she joined the Dan-Air fleet. She is seen here towards the end of her time with Dan-Air.

Dan-Air was not a typical charter airline, and its Comets reflected the difference with two large galleys to allow hot meals to be served to charter passengers for the first time. Shepherds' pie and sausage and mash were two favourite menu items.

In the mid-sixties Dan-Air had very little scheduled service traffic. Tour operators were willing to pay for hot food as a way of getting around ATLB rules which stated that inclusive holiday fares could not be lower than a standard air fare. Tour companies therefore bundled flights, hotels, meals, drinks, transfers, and excursions as part of a holiday in an effort to boost the fare up to the regular scheduled airfare.

The Comet 4Bs had a relatively short life with Dan-Air, but a useful one, forming the backbone of the airline's Comet fleet for much of the 1970s. In 1973, the 20-strong fleet flew a total of 15,001 flights, totalling 27,893 hours.

The aircraft shown was withdrawn from use in November 1977 and flown to Lasham, where she was subsequently scrapped in April 1978.

G-APMG is pictured here in Dan-Air's second livery, with a grey lower fuselage, a black 'underline' below the red cheatline and an all-red tail fin, with the company logo in a superimposed white disc. That logo consisted of a swallow-tailed flag of six vertical white and red stripes, the final red stripe being the depth of the cut in the swallowtail, with a four-pointed compass star. The registration was moved from the tail to the rear fuselage.

The airline name was presented on the aircraft as Dan-Air London to avoid any perception that it might be a Danish airline.

BELOW: **Like 14 of the 18 Comet 4Bs built, G-APMG initially served with BEA. The aircraft was then one of ten to serve with BEA Airtours, as seen here, and one of 12 of the type to fly with Dan-Air.** (Ian Joslin)

The Ultimate Comet

The 23 Comet 4Cs (and five similar RAF Comet C.Mk 4s) were the most impressive examples of the type, combining capacity with performance.

RIGHT: Only two Comet 4Cs flew in Misrair markings, as the airline changed its name to United Arab Airlines before the third aircraft in the order even flew! SU-ALC, seen here, was lost in a fatal accident on January 2, 1971, hitting sand dunes on approach to Tripoli in poor visibility.

BELOW: Compania Mexicana de Aviacion was the first customer for the final civil Comet variant, the Comet 4C. Here G-AOVU (soon to be XA-NAR) gets smartly airborne from a murky Hatfield, where the aircraft made her maiden flight on October 31, 1959.

The last Comet 4 variant, the Comet 4C, was, by some calculations, the most popular Comet variant. It was certainly the most impressive, combining the operating economies of the Comet 4B with the payload range capability of the Comet 4. The aircraft was referred to in contemporary de Havilland marketing literature as the 'Intermediate Comet 4C' because it combined features from the 'Intercontinental Comet 4' and the 'Continental Comet 4B'.

The Comet 4C combined the longer fuselage of the Comet 4B with the longer wings and extra fuel tanks of the original Comet 4, which gave it a longer range than the 4B, with the same payload and performance. The new variant could carry 106 passengers over a range of 2,820 miles and retained the excellent handling and superb field performance of previous Comet variants.

As a result, the Comet 4C was ordered by Mexicana, Middle East Airlines, Misrair (later United Arab Airlines), Sudan Airways, and Kuwait Airways. A single example was also delivered to Aerolíneas Argentinas as an attrition replacement, and another was supplied to the King of Saudi Arabia.

Whether or not the Comet 4C was, in fact, the most widely built Comet variant is the subject of some debate, and the answer depends upon which aircraft are included. De Havilland built 28 Comet 4s (the other claimant), and either 24, 29, 30 or 31 Comet 4Cs, depending how certain aircraft were counted!

Some 24 aircraft designated Comet 4C were produced and delivered to customers, plus five similar C.Mk 4s for the RAF. Two more were unsold, one making a single flight to Woodford as a Comet 4C prior to its conversion as the HS801 Nimrod prototype, the other being converted to Nimrod standards at Chester and never flying as a Comet 4C at all.

But whatever production total you personally endorse, there can be no doubt that the Comet 4C was the Comet's principal export variant, and no other version was ordered after it had been announced in late 1957.

ABOVE: **This Comet 4C was one of three destroyed by Israeli forces on the night of December 28, 1968, when eight commando-carrying Israeli helicopters attacked Beirut International Airport, leaving 13 Arab airliners wrecked by explosive charges placed in their undercarriage wells.**

And while a production total of fewer than 35 aircraft was unlikely to leave Boeing quaking with fear, it was an achievement. The basic Comet design was, by then, more than a decade old, and the Comet 4C had to compete with bigger, faster aircraft like the Boeing 707 and DC-8, more frugal twin jets like the Sud Caravelle, and a new generation of jetliners.

That it did so is a remarkable tribute to the fundamental 'rightness' of the design. Like other Comet variants, the Comet 4C was attractively priced, could operate from hot and high airfields and relatively short runways, and a single aircraft could fly more than 125m seat miles in the space of a single year.

COMPLICATED PRICING

Setting a competitive price for the Comet 4C was complicated by the agreements made between de Havilland and BOAC. De Havilland were endeavouring to sell a further 18 aircraft and were trying to negotiate a price of £1.05m per aircraft. But under the terms of BOAC's contract, de Havilland would have had to refund the

corporation £110,000 for each of BOAC's 19 Comet 4s, a total payment £2.09m. The managing director of De Havilland said that if BOAC insisted on its rights de Havilland might have to close down the production line, while BOAC's board maintained that in view of its previous heavy investment in the Comet programme, BOAC had to insist on its contractual rights. In May 1959, the government asked BOAC to waive its rights on the proposed Comet 4C sale to Pan Am affiliate Compania Mexicana de Aviacion – 'in the national interest'.

De Havilland claimed that the Comet variant that was being sold to CMA was substantially different from BOAC's model and that therefore they were not liable for any payment to the corporation, even if it was sold at a lower price than BOAC had paid for its Comet 4s. BOAC disagreed but in view of the minister's letter and the appeal to the 'national interest', the board acceded to the request without prejudice to the corporation's rights in any future sales.

in February 1960, de Havilland again sought release from the 'Most Favoured Customer clause', this time in respect to all sales of Comet 4B and 4C. There was considerable legal uncertainty as to whether the contract provision would apply to these types, and BOAC reluctantly accepted the inevitable – opening the way for de Havilland to sell new Comets for just £1.05 million each. Orders started to flow in!

There was no prototype for the Comet 4C and the first Comet 4C production aircraft (G-AOVU, later XA-NAR), destined for eventual service with Mexicana, made its five hour maiden flight on October 31, 1959, in the hands of Pat Fillingham, and in full Mexicana markings.

The aircraft had originally been laid down as a BOAC Comet 4, before being reallocated as a BEA Comet 4B, and finally as the first Comet 4C. After completing company test flying and flying in support of the type's certificate of airworthiness, the aircraft was used for route-proving and a South American demonstration tour.

Re-registered as XA-NAR, the aircraft was flown to Mexico City on June 8, 1960, and entered service with Mexicana that year. The aircraft was subsequently used as the test aircraft for US Federal Aviation Authority certification, which was obtained at Mexicana's request.

RIGHT: **Comet 4C ST-AAW is seen here in the final livery worn by Sudan Airways' Comets, with the new national flag on the tailfin. The airline's markings changed significantly while the Comet was in use, not least in going from a blue cheatline to a yellow one.** (Chris England)

ABOVE: This Chester-built Comet 4C served with Kuwait Airways until leased to MEA as a replacement for one of the aircraft destroyed in a supposedly retaliatory commando raid on Beirut airport. She eventually found herself flying for Dan-Air, serving until 1977.

BELOW: SU-ALE is seen here after the take-off accident at Munich on February 9, 1970, that led to her being written off. The captain aborted the take off after getting airborne and the aircraft went through the overshoot and the boundary fence before sliding to a halt. All those on board survived. (Manfred Kaffine)

The US assessment method allowed the Comet to operate at slightly higher take-off and landing weights than the British certification, and a few minor modifications were introduced, mainly to suit US operating procedures.

Mexicana went on to take delivery of three Comet 4Cs in January, June, and November 1960, which it later augmented with a pair of ex-BOAC Comet 4s in 1964 and 1965. The Comets were configured to carry 22 first class and 64 tourist class passengers, and operated so-called 'Golden Aztec' services, principally to Los Angeles, San Antonio, Chicago, and Havana. Comet services were constrained by Mexicana's financial problems, which also resulted in two further Comet 4Cs being cancelled. The Comet 4Cs were eventually retired in December 1970.

MIDDLE EAST

Following the re-opening of diplomatic relations between Egypt and the UK, Misrair signed a £4m contract for three Comet 4Cs on December 30, 1959, and two aircraft were delivered in June 1960 - SU-ALC on June 10, and SU-ALD on June 29. These were used to operate five weekly return services between Cairo and London, usually with a stop at one other city for traffic reasons – with Geneva, Zurich, and Frankfurt the chosen stops. Services were then added to Jeddah and Khartoum.

Misrair merged with Syrian Airways to form United Arab Airlines in 1960, and subsequent deliveries were in the amended livery. UAA was part of an innovative spares pooling arrangement with BOAC, BEA, Olympic Airways, MEA, and UAA with spares held at Cairo, Frankfurt, Khartoum, and Jeddah, London and Rome, Zurich, Geneva, and Beirut.

SU-ALE was delivered on December 23, 1960, and Egypt's President, Colonel Nasser used one of the Comet 4Cs for a visit to the UN in September 1960.

Four more were delivered between June 1961 and April 1962, and after two aircraft were lost in accidents, two attrition replacements followed in December 1962 and February 1964. The latter aircraft, SU-ANI, was the last Comet airliner to be delivered to a customer.

UAA became EgyptAir in 1969 and phased the Comets onto domestic routes, before finally withdrawing the type from service in 1976.

Middle East Airlines took delivery of four Comet 4Cs in 1960 and 1961, starting with OD-ADR, delivered on December 19, 1960. An option on a fifth aircraft was not taken up, though it was fully painted up in MEA markings and appeared at the 1961 Farnborough Air Show. The Comets were used on routes to Europe and the Indian sub-continent, and BOAC aircraft were leased on a number of occasions to increase capacity.

An Israeli commando attack on Beirut airport on December 28, 1968 destroyed three of MEA's Comets (OD-ADQ, OD-ADR, OD-ADS). The remaining aircraft, OD-ADT, continued to fly until October 1973 augmented by two Comet 4Cs (9K-ACA, 9K-ACE) and a Comet 4 (9K-ACI) leased from Kuwait Airways.

Another Middle Eastern airline that found the Comet 4C a compelling proposition was Sudan Airways, which took delivery of two Comet 4Cs that had originally been intended for Mexicana. ST-AAX was delivered on December 21, 1962, with ST-AAW following on January 11, 1963. The aircraft helped the airline establish and grow a small international route network, and were also used as VIP transports, when required. Sudan Airways retired the Comets from service at the end of 1972.

Aerolíneas Argentinas took delivery of a single Comet 4C (LV-AIB) on April 27, 1962, to augment its Comet 4s. The aircraft had been built for MEA, but the order had been cancelled.

JET EXPERIENCE

The last Comet 4C airline customer was Kuwait Airways, which ordered a pair of Comet 4Cs in order to gain jet experience, prior to delivery of the Trident 1E. Kuwait Airways thereby became the last new airline customer for the Comet 4. 9K-ACA was delivered on January 18, 1963, with 9K-ACE following on February 2, 1964. The airline used the Comets to inaugurate a service to London with stopovers at Geneva, Frankfurt, and Paris,

and later to operate services to Cairo, Beirut, Doha, Karachi, and Bombay.

In 1965 it added an ex-BOAC Comet 4, G-APDG (9K-ACI), to its fleet.

Kuwait retired the aircraft in 1968, although they were brought back into service later that year and leased to Middle Eastern Airlines. They only served MEA until March 1969 when they were again withdrawn from service and stored at Beirut awaiting sale.

Relatively few of the 21 airline Comet 4Cs went on to fly with a second operator. Westernair of Albuquerque purchased the three Mexicana aircraft, and tried to sell them on as a package, with spares and a simulator, unfortunately without

success. Dan-Air purchased ten Comet 4Cs in total. But most were scrapped at Lasham after spares recovery and Dan-Air flew just four of these – the ex-Aerolineas Argentinas aircraft, the two from Kuwait Airways and one of the Sudanese Comet 4Cs. This aircraft, ST-AAX, was re-registered as G-BDIF and remained in service until November 1979, making it Dan Air's last serving 'civilian' Comet!

There were two further proper Comet 4Cs – one delivered to the Saudi Royal Flight, one to the A&AEE at Boscombe Down, and the five RAF Comet C.Mk 4s. This left the two unsold Comet 4Cs that were converted to become the prototypes for the HS801 Nimrod. All of these aircraft are covered in other chapters.

ABOVE: This former RAF Comet C.Mk 4, G-BDIX, is seen in Dan-Air's final Comet livery, with the cheatline boldly outlined in black. The aircraft made the final Dan-Air Comet on September 30, 1981, to its new home at the Scottish Museum of Flight at East Fortune, whose runway was extended to allow the aircraft to land! (Ian Joslin)

LEFT: The World's last flying Comet was the A&AEE flying laboratory, XS235. She was a popular machine, despite frequent fuel leaks, but was finally withdrawn in 1997, to save the cost of a major overhaul.

de Havilland DH.106 Comet 4C
Comet 4C, XA-NAT, MEA

c/n 06443, **Fate:** Probably extant at a children's playground

Originally registered as G-ARBB, this Comet was delivered to Mexicana at Mexico City on November 29, 1960 and was re-registered as XA-NAT and named *Golden Knight*. The delivery flight was captained by captain Roberto Pini, and the distance of 5,880 miles was covered in just over 15 hours.

Mexicana was the first customer for the Comet 4C and signed a US$14m contract for three Comet 4Cs for delivery in 1960. The initial pair of aircraft needed to meet the Mexicana contract were originally intended to become two Comet 4Bs destined for BEA, but they were completed as the first and second Comet 4Cs to speed up delivery. XA-NAT was the last of this trio.

Mexicana did not exercise its option on two further Comet 4Cs which were instead sold to Sudan Airways but did instead purchase two former BOAC Comet 4s in 1965.

Mexicana's first colour scheme used an unusual twin blue cheatline, with 'MEXICANA' titles in gold on the forward fuselage. Subsequently, a solid blue cheatline was used, initially with 'MEXICANA' in blue, and later 'mexicana' in black as shown here.

From 1969, a new livery was introduced, with a gold cheatline and a stylised eagle's head logo on the fin, using the same italicised, lower case 'mexicana' titles. *Golden Aztec* was painted on the starboard pinion tank, with *Azteca de Oro* to port, throughout these livery changes.

The Mexicana Comet fleet (including XA-NAT) was dormant from 1970 and was traded in for Boeing 727s in 1972, though the Comets remained with Mexicana who were at liberty to dispose of the Comets however they could. In April 1973 Westernair of Albuquerque, New Mexico purchased all three Mexicana Comets and began refurbishing them. XA-NAT was refurbished and registered as N777WA but remained at Mexico City Airport, where she was eventually sold to the Parque Hidalgo Zoo. Initially intended to be used as a restaurant, the aircraft was broken up in 1980, the fuselage then serving as a cafe.

BELOW: **Aerovias Guest S.A. was Mexico's third airline and had been founded after Mexicana de Aviación and Aeronaves de Mexico. Guest replaced their Super Constellations on the Mexico City-Paris route with two Comet 4Cs (XA-NAR and XA-NAT) which were leased from Mexicana. This aircraft shows off the original Mexicana scheme, with its twin cheatline and gold titles.**

de Havilland DH.106 Comet 4C
Comet 4C, OD-ADT, MEA

c/n 06450, **Fate:** Scrapped at Lasham June 1974

Carrying the Cedar of Lebanon on its tail fin, this Comet 4C (OD-ADT) was the final aircraft in a £5.25m order for four Comets for Middle East Airlines.

The Lebanese carrier used a similar scheme to BOAC, albeit with red cheatlines instead of blue, and with a white tail fin. Its Comets were known as 'Cedar Jets'. MEA had been established with operational and technical support from BOAC in 1945, though management was initially provided by Pan Am. BOAC bought the American airline's 49% stake in Middle East Airlines in 1955, and pumped money into the ailing carrier. The company's debts were such that Her Majesty's Treasury initially refused approval for the Comet buy sought by MEA chairman Sheikh Najib Alamuddin. After a threat to buy Caravelles, the issue was smoothed over, and MEA ordered four Comet 4Cs.

Before taking delivery of their own aeroplanes, from November 1960 until March 1961, MEA chartered two Comet services from BOAC on the Beirut to London and Dhahran routes in order to assess operational procedures.

This aircraft was built in Chester and made its maiden flight on March 9, 1961 and was delivered to Middle East Airlines nine days later.

At one time, MEA's chairman said that he felt that a new Trident had no real advantage over a well-amortized Comet. "The cost of operating the Comet was a little higher but was definitely compensated for by their excellent performance," he said.

Three of the four Middle Eastern Airlines' Comets (OD-ADS, OD-ADR, OD-ADQ) were among 13 aircraft destroyed at Beirut Airport by Israeli commandos on the night of December 28, 1968. OD-ADT survived the attack and continued to serve until October 1973 when it was finally sold to Dan-Air Services Ltd. The survivor was augmented by two Kuwait Airways Comets which were leased to boost MEA's capacity.

The surviving original MEA aircraft was flown from Gatwick to Lasham for spare parts on October 4, 1973, landing with 31,082 hours and 23,877 flights 'on the clock'. She was finally scrapped at Lasham in June 1974.

BELOW: **OD-ADT basks in the sun in front of the brutalist architecture of BOAC's main hangar at Heathrow! The MEA scheme later evolved to incorporate 'Middle East Airlines – Air Liban' titles in English and Arabic, and a 'wings' logo on the nose.** (Caz Caswell)

de Havilland DH.106 Comet 4C
Comet 4C, ST-AAX, Sudan Airways

c/n 06463, **Fate:** Scrapped at Lasham October 1980

Sudan Airways purchased two Comets in 1962. ST-AAW flew on November 5, 1962, and joined Sudanese independence celebrations in Khartoum on November 16, having been diverted from pre-delivery flights. It was then returned to Hatfield for the completion of testing and was finally delivered to Sudan Airways in January 1963. ST-AAX was delivered to Sudan Airways at London Airport on December 21, 1962, after undertaking a promotional tour taking in Khartoum, Cairo, Beirut, and Athens.

The Sudanese Comets entered service wearing a colour scheme with a pale blue cheat line dividing the white top from the highly polished undersides. 'SUDAN AIRWAYS' titles in Arabic and English were applied above the cheat line, flanking the original blue, yellow and green Sudanese national flag, with Arabic forward and English aft. The yellow tail fin had 'SUDAN AIRWAYS' written on it to port with a stylised Sudan Airways badge to starboard.

The aircraft later gained a blue-edged yellow cheat line with the national flag above the cheat line flanked by 'SUDAN AIRWAYS' in English forward and in Arabic aft. The Sudan Airways badge was applied in a white oval on each side of the tail fin. Finally, the old national flag was replaced by the Sudan Airways badge above the cheatline, with a large representation of the new red, white, black, and green national flag applied to the tail fin.

Servicing of the Sudanese Comets was transferred from BEA to MEA in Beirut in late 1968. Sudan Airways retired its Comets from service at the end of 1972. ST-AAW was flown to Teesside for storage on November 14, 1972, while ST-AAX remained in Khartoum. Dan-Air purchased the two Comets in 1975. ST-AAW was flown to Lasham on August 1, 1975 and was scrapped 14 months later. ST-AAX was flown to Lasham on July 7, 1975 and entered service with Dan-Air as G-BDIF in August 1975. The aircraft flew its last service on November 5, 1979, which made it Dan-Air's final serving 'civilian' Comet! The aircraft was scrapped in October 1980.

BELOW: **ST-AAW was the sister ship of the aircraft illustrated above, and is seen here in Sudan Airways' early livery, with the old national flag on the fuselage above the cheatline, and with the airline's stylised badge on the tailfin. The cheatline was originally blue.** (Tony Clarke Collection via David Whitworth)

de Havilland DH.106 Comet 4C
Comet 4C, SU-ALM, EgyptAir

c/n 06458, **Fate:** Scrapped at Lasham 1977, nose survives at North East Aircraft Museum

SU-ALM was one of four Comet 4Cs operated by EgyptAir and is seen here in the interim UAA/EgyptAir scheme used in the early 1970s.

Egypt's Misrair signed a £4m contract for three Comet 4Cs in December 1959. Only the first two aircraft wore '*MISRAIR*' titles, the third being delivered with '*UNITED ARAB AIRLINES*' titles. The colour scheme was essentially the same, with the Egyptian flag on the tail fin, and a smart green cheatline, consisting of a narrow pinstripe between two broader stripes, with '*UNITED ARAB AIRLINES*' in place of the original '*MISRAIR*'. United Arab Airlines (UAA) ordered two more aircraft in January 1961, three more in 1962 and one more in February 1964.

The UAA Comets were occasionally used as Presidential transports by Gamal Abdel Nasser Hussein, Egypt's leader from 1956 until his death in 1970.

By the end of January 1971, when UAA became EgyptAir, the airline still had four Comets (SU-ALL, SU-ALM, SU-ALV and SU-ANC), one more (SU-ALC) having been written off that month before it could be repainted.

The basic Misrair/UAA colour scheme was used on at least two of the four Comets after the name change, though the new airline did soon adopt a new colour scheme, with a broad red cheat line and a narrower bronze one below it. The flag on the tail was replaced by a new logo, a falcon's head that represented Horus, the ancient Egyptian 'winged god of the sun', who was usually depicted as a falcon or a man with the head of a falcon.

EgyptAir withdrew its surviving Comets from service in 1975 and 1976 and they were then purchased by Dan-Air. Three aircraft were flown to Lasham to be used for spares while the last was stripped for spares at Cairo.

SU-ALM made the last EgyptAir Comet flight on March 30, 1976, and was sold to Dan-Air on October 14, before being ferried to Lasham as G-BEEX. The nose was sold to BAe at Woodford for Nimrod trials work, and eventually found its way to the North East Aircraft Museum at Sunderland. The nose remains at Sunderland to this day, still in EgyptAir's bright red and gold colours.

BELOW: **SU-ALM ended her days, like so many Comet 4s, 4Bs and 4Cs, being scrapped at Lasham. By the time the aircraft arrived at the Hampshire airfield, it was wearing EgyptAir's final livery, with a red cheatline and a falcon's head tail badge.** (Alan Pratt)

de Havilland DH.106 Comet 4C
Comet 4C, 9K-ACE, Kuwait Airways

c/n 06474, **Fate:** Scrapped at Lasham c.1978 after service with Dan-Air

This Comet 4C, 9K-ACE, was one of the last aircraft built, being the penultimate aircraft to be delivered to an airline customer. She is shown here in the livery of Kuwait Airways. She made her first flight from the de Havilland factory airfield at Chester on December 17, 1963, flying to Hatfield for production testing. Purchased by Kuwait Airways, 9K-ACE was delivered to Kuwait on February 2, 1964.

Kuwait had two Comet 4Cs (9K-ACA and 9K-ACE) which it used on routes to London, Paris, Frankfurt, Doha, Karachi, and Bombay. On July 4, 1964 one of Kuwait Airways Comet's was involved in an unusual incident when captain Dennis Deacon was forced to turn back to Cairo after a flight attendant informed him that a fight had broken out in the cabin. Two sheikhs were involved in a fight after one of them touched a baby with his foot as he went down the gangway and the father took exception to this. The fight soon escalated and a further 60 sheikhs, emirs and members of their families became involved. After several people were removed from the flight the aircraft proceeded on its way.

The aircraft served Kuwait Airways for almost five years and was then leased to MEA (Middle Eastern Airlines) on January 19, 1969. 9K-ACE returned to Kuwait Airways in July 1969 and was finally withdrawn from service that September. The aircraft was placed in storage at Beirut having flown 6,899 flights totalling 14,336 flying hours. It was not flown for the rest of 1969 and 1970.

On March 20, 1971, 9K-ACE was sold to Dan-Air and was flown from Beirut to Lasham where she was refurbished. The aircraft entered service with Dan-Air on May 30, 1971 as G-AYVS and flew for the airline for seven years. The aircraft made its last passenger flight on January 4, 1977 and made a final flight to Lasham two days later, completing a total of 25,011 flying hours and 11,234 flights.

BELOW: **Kuwait Airways was the final airline customer for the Comet 4C, taking two aircraft while waiting for the delivery of its Tridents. The aircraft were subsequently leased to MEA to replace aircraft destroyed by the Israeli army in 1968.**

de Havilland DH.106 Comet 4C
Comet 4C, G-BDIV, Dan-Air

c/n 06469, **Fate:** Scrapped at Lasham July 1985

Dan-Air's final Comets were five former RAF Comet C.Mk 4s, including the former XR397, seen here in Dan-Air's final colour scheme, with a broad black outline to the red cheatline, and a black fin leading edge.

The RAF Comet C.Mk 4s (equivalent to the civil Comet 4C) were prematurely retired in June and July 1975, as a result of defence cuts that decimated the RAF's transport force, alongside the service's remaining Argosies, Belfasts, and Britannias. The Comets were in excellent condition, with relatively low flying hours, and at a unit price of £120,000 represented an unmissable opportunity for Dan-Air.

These aircraft were to be the last operational Comets Dan-Air purchased, though the company subsequently purchased four Comet 4Cs from Egyptair in October 1976 for spares use. The five ex-RAF Comets were registered G-BDIT, G-BDIU, G-BDIV, G-BDIW and G-BDIX (formerly XR395, '96, '97, '98 and '99 respectively). Initially configured for 109 passengers they were later modified to carry 119 - the maximum number of passengers the Comet ever carried. The aircraft allowed a significant increase in flying hours by the fleet, although economics were rapidly swinging against the gas-guzzling

Comet, which returned half the number of passenger seat miles per kilogram of fuel compared to the Boeing 727, for example.

Despite this, utilisation rates continued to increase during the mid-1970s. For the 1977 season Dan-Air were using nine 4Bs and nine 4Cs. The Comet fleet accumulated 17,217 hours for the 1975 season and 23,123 hours in 1977. The seasonal nature of the Inclusive Tour (IT) market meant very high flying rates 'in season' - with around 360 hours per aircraft per month, but also allowed the winter lay-off period to be used for maintenance.

G-BDIV retired in November 1979, with 15,911 flying hours behind her, and the four remaining ex-RAF aircraft flew the Comet's last full season for Dan-Air in 1980, with all Comet services having ceased by November 1980.

G-BDIV was briefly preserved as part of Dan-Air's own collection of historic aircraft but was broken up in 1985.

BELOW: **G-BDIW was a sister aircraft of G-BDIV illustrated above. The ex-RAF Comet C.Mk 4 is seen here at Bristol Airport, wearing Dan-Air's second Comet colour scheme. The RAF Comet 4s were the last Comets to fly in airline service.** (Chris England)

Comet In Uniform

After the first generation Comet 'crashed and burned' as a commercial airliner, military operators ensured its rehabilitation.

RIGHT: **A 412 Squadron Comet 1XB wearing the final RCAF Comet livery, with a twin cheatline running through the windows and the Canadian Red Ensign on the tailfin. This gave way to the familiar Maple leaf flag in 1965, after the Comet's retirement.** (Caz Caswell)

BELOW: **Two Comets at a USAF air base. The furthest aircraft is XK669, the first Comet T.Mk 2, and wears an unusual livery, with the cheatline running below the cabin windows. This seems to have been a feature of the T.Mk 2s when they entered service.**

The Royal Canadian Air Force (RCAF) formulated a requirement for two high-speed transport and VIP aircraft in 1951. In October 1952, after inspecting the Comet, the RCAF placed an order for two aircraft.

The following month, two full RCAF flight crews (each with a pilot, co-pilot, navigator, flight engineer and radio officer and two cabin crew) were sent to England to receive familiarisation training on the Comets. These were officially handed over to the RCAF on March 18 and April 13, 1953, and flew over 100 training hours, including international flights to Johannesburg and Singapore. The first aircraft and crew returned to Canada on May 29, 1953, and joined No.412 Squadron, alongside the unit's Beechcraft Expeditor Mk.3s, Canadair North Stars, Canadair CC-106 Yukons, Canadair CC-109 Cosmopolitans, Douglas Dakota Mk.IIIs & IVs, and North American Mitchell Mk.IIIs. The RCAF thereby became the first air force in the world to operate jet transports.

The main role of the Comets was to fly 'high priority' Canadian military personnel and their dependents to and from Europe – those with a lower priority flying by North Star or going by sea! The Comets also provided high altitude target services for Canadian fighter aircraft and exercising Air Defence Command and NORAD, simulating Russian jet bombers.

At any given time, 412 Squadron operated with four complete Comet crews.

The RCAF Comets were withdrawn from service in January 1954 after the series of crashes that grounded the commercial Comet fleet. The two RCAF Comets were initially stored at de Havilland's Canadian factory at Downsview, Toronto from April 1954.

After the British court of enquiry, it was decided that the Comets should be re-built with heavier gauge skins, and the two aircraft were therefore ferried unpressurised back to Broughton, Chester for rebuild to Comet 1XB standards. This saw them gain elliptical windows, a further reinforced

fuselage structure and modified wing leading edges. The aircraft were fitted with uprated Ghost Mk.4 engines and the jet pipes were swept outward to reduce the stresses on the fuselage. The cost of the modification was put at £142,000.

In August 1957, crews from 412 Squadron proceeded to Hatfield for re-familiarisation and flight training. The group included nine pilots, five navigators and three radio officers.

After initial flights throughout the United Kingdom and into Germany, the two RCAF aircraft flew from Hatfield to Johannesburg, routeing via Rome, El Adem, Khartoum, Entebbe, and Salisbury. The aircraft then returned to Hatfield before returning to Canada and resuming service on November 1, 1957.

The Comets made their last scheduled flights into Marville on March 1, 1962, after which the CC-106 Yukon took over the schedule completely. The Comets continued to fly into Marville on unscheduled missions, and the very last flight that was flown to Marville took place on August 8, 1963. The two Comets were retired from 412 Squadron service on October 10, 1964 and were ferried to the Aircraft Maintenance and Disposal Unit (AMDU) at RCAF Station Mountain View on October 30, 1964 where they were officially 'struck off strength'.

One aircraft was sold to Mr. Eldon Armstrong on July 30, 1965, and the other was scrapped. The aircraft was flown to No.6 Repair Deport at Trenton where it was repainted blue and white with the civilian registration CF-SVR, before being ferried to Mount Hope airport (in Hamilton) where it was periodically started and taxied.

RAF COMET

While Canada had made a quite deliberate decision to acquire the Comet as a military jet transport, the type's second military user became a customer almost by chance. Though the Royal Air Force might well have selected the Comet for service eventually, to meet a formally issued requirement, that is not how it came to acquire the Comet C.Mk 2.

Various Comet iterations were put forward in response to requirement C.132/OR.315, alongside offerings from Avro, Handley Page, Shorts, and Vickers. The so-called Stage 1 Comet was based on the BOAC Comet 1 then under development, while the Stage 2 lacked RATOG.

The Stage 3 was Avon-engined, and Stage 4 (later known as the 'Developed Comet') had Rolls Royce Conway engines. The competition soon became a two-horse race between the Developed Comet and the Vickers V.1000, with the latter eventually being selected, before being cancelled in late 1952 in favour of the turboprop Britannia.

Despite this, the RAF would end up receiving a jet transport, this time in the shape of the Comet 2! With BOAC and other airline customers cancelling their Comet 2 orders in the wake of the losses of G-ALYP and G-ALYY, and the subsequent withdrawal of the type's certificate of airworthiness, the British government decided to buy some of the suddenly superfluous Comet 2s for use by the Royal Air Force.

Three were acquired as SIGINT platforms, as described in the next chapter, but more were purchased as transport aircraft. The Ministry of Supply purchased 14 Comet 2 airframes (c/ns 06023-06032, 06034-06037 and 06045) on March 18, 1955 – the first four of which were already flying in BOAC markings, with the rest taking shape on the production line. Three were allocated for conversion to Comet 2R standards (06023, 06025 and 06027), and one (06026, G-AMXD) became a Comet 2E, and was initially used to support the Comet 4 development programme.

RIGHT: Comet C.Mk 2 XK669 *Taurus* with three of 216 Squadron's new Comet C.Mk 4s in a photo that clearly shows the longer fuselage of the later variant, as well as the pinion tanks mounted on the wing leading edge.

The remaining ten aircraft were converted as military transports, first receiving a package of modifications similar to that applied to produce the Comet 1XB, with thicker fuselage skins, rip-stop doublers, elliptical windows, and other improvements. This was to ensure that the aircraft could be operated pressurised, while still obtaining a full commercial passenger-carrying certificate of airworthiness – a vital confidence-building measure for the RAF.

De Havilland completed one aircraft (c/n 06036) to the full, planned RAF standard, and this airframe was then subjected to fatigue and pressurisation testing in a newly-built water tank at Hatfield, before production began. Three more incomplete airframes (c/ns 06039, 06040, and 06047) were cocooned and stored as 'fleet reserves'.

G-AMXB (c/n 06024) and the almost complete G-AMXF (c/n 06028) were stripped of their BOAC colours and converted to virtually the full RAF standard, lacking only the full-standard strengthened floor. Designated as T.Mk 2s, and serialled XK669 and XK670, the two aircraft were delivered to RAF Lyneham on June 7 (XK670) and June 8 (XK669), 1956. The T.Mk 2s were detached to Boscombe Down for service trials and for the compilation of Pilots' Notes.

Aircrew training began immediately, with pilots completing a Comet conversion course that consisted of 55 hours of day flying and 20 hours of night-flying (this included 18 hours as P2, 17 hours in command, and 40 hours of screened route flying). At the end of the course, pilots were granted a Transport Command Passenger Carrying C category.

The first operational Comet flight by 216 Squadron was made by T.Mk 2 XK670, which carried the secretary of state for sir and senior RAF officers to Moscow Airport on June 23, 1956 to allow them to attend the Air Display at Tushino Airport. In the process, XK670 became the first British jet-engined aircraft to visit the Russian capital. The aircraft brought its VIP passengers home and then returned to Moscow some days later, on July 3, to conduct a demonstration flight.

Scheduled flights to Singapore began in June 1956 and the route was soon extended to Adelaide and Brisbane marking the beginning of full scale Comet C.Mk 2 operations. In early November, 216 Squadron flew equipment to Malta and Cyprus to support operations at Suez.

The first full-standard Comet C.Mk 2 was XK671 (c/n 06029), delivered to Boscombe Down for clearance testing on August 21, 1956. She joined 216 Squadron at Lyneham on October 16, joining XK695 (delivered on September

BELOW: The RAF's Comets flew missions in support of Operation *Musketeer* (the Suez operation), including Casevac flights from Malta and Cyprus.

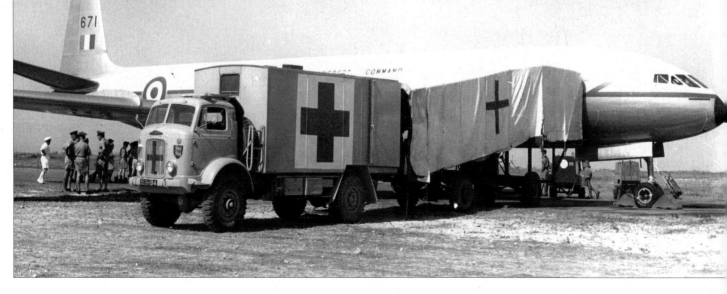

1956). Six further C.Mk 2s followed over the next six months, and the tenth and final C.Mk 2 aircraft built, XK716, was delivered on May 7, 1957, the last Comet for the squadron. It was the first Comet (and the only Comet 2) built at Chester. Subsequently, the two T.Mk 2s were brought to the same standard. XK670 was converted to full C.Mk 2 standards at Chester from November 1957 and XK669 from January 1958, and the two aircraft rejoined 216 Squadron in April and May 1958, bringing the strength up to ten C.Mk 2s.

TRANSATLANTIC

Soon 216 Squadron began flying across the Atlantic to North America and then on across the Pacific to Christmas Island. These included the first non-stop westbound crossings of the North Atlantic by any jet transport aircraft. Slip crews were placed at the staging posts to allow the original crew to rest while the Comet flew on. The squadron carried an assortment of high profile VIPs, including The Queen and Prince Philip, and US President Eisenhower and British Prime Minister Harold Macmillan. It was the first time that an American President had flown in a foreign aircraft.

The Comet C.Mk 2 proved to be an excellent medevac/ casevac aircraft, carrying six stretchers in three pairs in the forward cabin and sitting patients aft. The shorter flight times of the Comet could make the difference between life and death, and patients travelled in quiet, smooth, pressurised, air conditioned, humidified comfort!

The squadron's strength was reduced to nine aircraft in July 1961, when XK695 was sent for conversion to 2R standards for 51 Squadron. Another (XK671) was sent to 51 Squadron as a support aircraft in September 1962, following the delivery of five new C.Mk 4s between February and June 1962.

The Comet C.Mk 2 fleet started to draw down in January 1966, with the retirement of XK670. XK669 and XK715 followed in April 1966, and XK696 in October. This left four aircraft in service at the beginning of 1967. XK697 went to 51 Squadron in March, and XK669 and XK716 were withdrawn in April. The final aircraft, XK698, was withdrawn from service on June 9, 1967, and subsequently went into storage. The RAF's order for five Comet C.Mk 4s (based on the commercial Comet 4C), for delivery during 1961 and 1962, was announced on September 5, 1960.

The first aircraft, XR395, made its first flight to Hatfield on November 15, 1961, and was then delivered to the A&AEE at Boscombe Down in January 1962 for handling evaluation and preparation of the Pilots' Notes. XR395 was then delivered to 216 Squadron at RAF Lyneham on

June 1, 1962, with the second (XR396), though the others (XR397-399) had by then already been delivered.

RAF Transport Command initially used the new C.Mk 4s alongside the C.Mk 2s, using the new type primarily on its longer routes. The Comet C.Mk 4 could carry six pairs of stretchers and 47 seats in the Casevac role, and could be configured for VVIP use, with two beds, a VIP lounge/ dining room and 34 seats aft. Alternatively, there were high density layouts with 86 or 96 rear-facing seats, although, after the introduction of the VC10, the Comets were used primarily in the VIP role.

On June 30, 1975, 216 Squadron disbanded as part of a wider series of defence cuts which decimated the RAF's transport arm, and which saw the premature retirement of the remaining Andovers, Argosies, Britannias, and Belfasts. Between June 21 and 3 July, 1975, the five Comet C.Mk 4s were flown to No.60 MU at Leconfield to await disposal. In good condition and with low flying hours they were soon snapped up by Dan-Air.

The final government operator of the Comet was Saudi Arabia, which ordered a single Comet 4C for the nascent Saudi Royal Flight in September 1961. The aircraft was used for crew training at Hatfield during September and October 1962 and visited Saudi Arabia in October. The aircraft positioned at Geneva on March 19, 1963, before flying the King (Saud bin Abdulaziz al Saud) to Nice. The aircraft made a number of flights between Geneva and Nice, carrying members of the King's family and retinue, and during one such flight, on March 30, the aircraft flew into a mountainside in the Alps after descending below the altitude cleared by ATC.

ABOVE: **By 1975, the Comet C.Mk 4s were assigned to Strike Command and wore plain 'ROYAL AIR FORCE' titles. Undersides were painted light aircraft grey.**

BELOW: **A single Comet 4C was delivered to the Saudi Royal Flight in June 1962, wearing this distinctive colour scheme. The aircraft was lost nine months later.** (Caz Caswell)

de Havilland DH.106 Comet 1A
Comet 1A, 5301, 412 Squadron, RCAF

c/n 06017, **Fate:** Scrapped at Mountain View October 1965, nose to National Aviation Museum, Rockcliffe

The Royal Canadian Air Force placed an order for two de Havilland Comet 1As in November 1951, with the intention of using the aircraft to replace lumbering, piston-engined Canadair North Star transports in RCAF Service, but also hoping to use the aircraft to test Canada's fighter forces and radar chain, simulating enemy jet bombers.

Two complete crews from 412 Squadron went to Hatfield for familiarisation training on the Comet in October 1952, and the first Comet was delivered to the UK detachment on March 14, 1953. The RCAF crews subsequently flew more than 100 flying hours on the Comet, including flights to Johannesburg and Singapore.

The first Comet, seen here, arrived at RCAF Station Uplands in Ottawa, on Friday, May 29, 1953. The RCAF Comets were delivered in a smart colour scheme with very highly polished undersides and a white fuselage top. This began from just below the cabin windows and extended forward over the upper part of the nose, but unusually the double red cheatline (broken by 'ROYAL CANADIAN AIR FORCE' titles), was initially located above the windows. For a very brief period, codes flanked the fuselage roundel, the first aircraft carrying OZ-301.

Its early adoption of the Comet made the RCAF the first air force in the world to operate a jet transport aircraft - stealing a march on Britain's Royal Air Force, and the US Air Force.

The Royal Canadian Air Force stuck with the Comet even after the grounding of the Comet 1s, getting its aircraft converted to Comet 1XB standards at Chester in 1957, and keeping them in service until 1963. On retirement, 5301 donated some spares to her sistership, and was then 'decapitated', her nose being saved for the National Aviation Museum at Rockcliffe in Ottawa, though she spent most of the next 50 years in store, or displayed in a corner, strapped to a trolley - a sad end for a distinguished and historic airframe that deserved much better.

BELOW: **The RCAF's first Comet, 5301, seen in her final guise as a Comet 1XB, wearing the later RCAF livery.**

de Havilland DH.106 Comet 1XB, 5302 (c/n 06018), No.412 Squadron, RCAF

de Havilland DH.106 Comet 1XB
Comet 1XB, 5302, 412 Squadron, RCAF

c/n 06018, **Fate:** Retired October 1963, scrapped Miami, 1975

This aircraft was the second of a pair of Comet 1As delivered to 412 Squadron on April 13, 1953, sister aircraft 5301 (c/n 06017) having been delivered on March 18. The unit thereby became the world's first military transport squadron.

The Royal Canadian Air Force's Comets were grounded in April 1954, following the loss of G-ALYY, and were placed in storage. Both were subsequently flown back across the Atlantic (unpressurised) for rebuild to Comet 1XB standards, with thicker fuselage skins, elliptical windows, and other improvements.

This Mk.1A was converted to Comet 1XB standards from July 1956 and was re-delivered in September 1957. By July 1958, the RCAF Comet colour scheme had been modified, with the cheat line lowered to window level (now the demarcation between the silver-painted undersides and the white top), but with the 'ROYAL CANADIAN AIR FORCE' titles retained on a silver bar above windows and cheatline. Soon afterwards, the red, white, and blue fin flash was replaced by the Canadian Red Ensign, which was then the national flag.

5302 served with 412 Squadron until October 3, 1963. She was ferried to Mountain View for storage on October 30 but was sold to one Eldon Armstrong for use as an executive transport in July 1965 and was flown to Mount Hope near Hamilton as CF-SVR. For its proposed role as an executive transport, this Comet 1XB was repainted with a pale blue cheat line, with an 'L'-shaped chevron in the same colour on the tail fin, applied above the new red and white maple leaf Canadian flag.

At Mount Hope the aircraft was started up and taxied around periodically but did not fly.

Sold to brokers B Dallas Airmotive in 1968, the aircraft was re-registered as N373S and was flown to Miami for proposed charter work, or, according to some reports, for onward sale to Peru. This failed to happen, and the aircraft was scrapped in 1975, after passing through the hands of four new owners, all of whom failed to get the aircraft flying.

BELOW: **The RCAF Comets initially wore the same 'delivery' colour scheme after their return from conversion to Comet 1XB standards – only the new oval windows giving the game away.**

de Havilland DH.106 Comet T.Mk 2
Comet T.Mk 2, XK669, 216 Squadron

c/n 06024, **Fate:** Nose to RAE Farnborough, 1969. Remainder burned on Lyneham's fire dump, 1970

XK669 was one of the first two Comets delivered to 216 Squadron of RAF Transport Command, based at Lyneham in Wiltshire. It had originally flown in BOAC markings as G-AMXB on March 11, 1953. The first two aircraft were delivered in June 1956 and operational flying began with a historic trip to Moscow to allow the secretary of state for air and senior officers to attend the air show at Tushino.

This aircraft, with XK670, was delivered to an interim standard, without the definitive strengthened cabin floor, and as such was designated as a T.Mk 2. Both T.Mk 2s were originally used for training and route-proving, though both were subsequently brought up to full C.Mk 2 standards.

Following the series of accidents that grounded the Comet 1 fleet, the Ministry of Supply had purchased 15 of the Comet 2s intended for BOAC on March 18, 1955. Of these aircraft, one was used only for structural testing of the planned RAF configuration, three were allocated for conversion as Comet 2R SIGINT aircraft for 192 Squadron, one was used as a Comet 2E to support Comet 4 development, and the remaining ten became Comet T.Mk 2 or C.Mk 2 transports for RAF Transport Command.

In RAF service, the Comet C.Mk 2s were generally finished with white upper surfaces and silver-painted or later polished aluminium or in a couple of cases, light grey undersides. Some of the earliest examples had their tail fins painted silver, but white tail fins were the norm. 'ROYAL AIR FORCE TRANSPORT COMMAND' titles were applied above the cheat line. A dark blue cheatline was usually applied at window level, with a 'zig zag' forward taking it under the cockpit to the nose radome, but the two Comet T.Mk 2s (XK669 and XK670) initially had a much lower cheatline, which ran below the cabin windows, and which initially appeared not to have a radome, but instead a plain white nose cap.

RIGHT AND BELOW: Some felt that the lowered cheatline on the Comet T.Mk 2 gave the aircraft a more modern look, but a more traditional livery was used on production C.Mk 2s. XK669 was initially used for loadmaster training after her retirement.

de Havilland DH.106 Comet C.Mk 2
Comet C.Mk 2, XK716, 216 Squadron

c/n 06045, **Fate:** Retired April 1967, scrapped 1973 after serving as a GI airframe at Halton

A handful of 216 Squadron's Comet C.Mk 2s, including XK697, XK715 and XK716 were decorated with dayglo noses and dayglo bands around the rear fuselage. These splashes of colour were apparently applied to ensure high visibility during the 1961 Berlin crisis, identifying them as transport aircraft to Russian fighters. On September 15, 1961, XK716 was deployed to Gutersloh where she was held on standby - ready to run the gauntlet and defy the ban, had Russia carried out its threat to close the Berlin corridor. Though they looked like training colours, the dayglo patches did not denote that the aircraft were T.Mk 2 aircraft, as has sometimes been reported.

XK716 was the first Comet to be built at Chester and was laid down as the first Comet 2 for UAT, even being part-painted in the French airline's distinctive colours. Work began on finishing the aircraft and converting it to C.Mk 2 standards in January 1956, and the final RAF paintwork was applied a year later. Unlike some earlier C.Mk 2s which had silver-painted undersides, XK716 had highly polished natural metal undersides.

XK716 made her first flight on May 6, 1957, from Broughton, leading to her becoming known as the 'First Welsh Comet'. The test flight culminated in a landing at Hatfield, which became standard practice for all future Chester-built Comets.

RIGHT AND BELOW: **While serving as a ground instructional airframe at Halton, XK716 donated her tailfin for the repair of RAE Bedford's Comet 3. The original fin was replaced by a newly-made wooden tailfin, for appearance's sake only!** (Reto Fasciatti via Urs Baettig -'Before' and Alan Allen 'After')

In service, XK716 flew the last scheduled RAF service from Ceylon on January 30, 1960, and flew many dignitaries, troops, and families during her career. She was named *Cepheus*, after the constellation in the northern sky, which was in turn named after Cepheus, a king of Aethiopia in Greek mythology. The name was painted on the nose, below and just behind the cockpit windows.

XK716 served with 216 Squadron until withdrawn from service in April 1967, making her final flight on May 4, 1967 to the grass airfield at RAF Halton, where she was used for apprentice training until scrapped in May 1973.

de Havilland DH.106 Comet C.Mk 4
Comet C.Mk 4, XR397, 216 Squadron

c/n 06469, **Fate:** Retired June 1975, sold to Dan-Air, scrapped at Lasham

The order for a batch of five Comet C.Mk 4s, based on the commercial Comet 4C, was announced at the 1961 Farnborough Air Show. The new variant was intended to 'bridge the gap' pending the service introduction of the BAC VC10.

The first RAF Comet C.Mk 4 was delivered to Boscombe Down in January 1962, and it was XR397, the third aircraft built, shown here, that actually became the first to be delivered to 216 Squadron on February 14, 1962. Unlike the Comet C.Mk 2s, the Comet C.Mk 4s were not individually named.

The new variant was configured to carry 94 passengers (compared to 44 on the C.Mk 2), though it normally carried 80, or, in a high-density trooping configuration, 96. Like all RAF transport aircraft at the time, the Comet C.Mk 4 used rearward-facing seats for better crashworthiness.

The Comet C.Mk 4 could be reconfigured to carry 12 stretchers with attendants, and 47 seated wounded in the Casevac role, and two of the aircraft could be rapidly reconfigured in a VIP layout, with two beds forward, a dining table and armchairs in a 'VIP' lounge compartment, and four further fully reclining 'sleeperette' seats. Further aft were 34 'standard' seats.

The Comet C.Mk 4s were used for longer range trips to the Far East, while the smaller C.Mk 2s flew shorter missions to the Mediterranean.

When first delivered, as shown here, the Comet C.Mk 4 was finished with white upper surfaces and natural metal, unpainted undersides. 'ROYAL AIR FORCE TRANSPORT COMMAND' titles were applied above the cheatline.

This aircraft was withdrawn from use on June 17, 1975, prior to the disbandment of 216 Squadron on the last day of the month. She had flown 11,339 flying hours. With her sisters, XR397 was briefly stored at No.60 MU, RAF Leconfield, before being purchased by Dan-Air in August. The aircraft flew with Dan-Air as G-BDIV (as shown on page 79) until of the end of the 1980 season, subsequently becoming the last Comet to be scrapped at Lasham.

BELOW: **XR397, the subject of the artwork above, is seen here later in her career, fresh from a major overhaul and repaint into the smart grey and white colour scheme applied during the Comet C.Mk 4s final three years of RAF service.** (Chris England)

de Havilland DH.106 Comet C.Mk 4
Comet C.Mk 4, XR399, 216 Squadron

c/n 06471, **Fate:** Retired June 1975, sold to Dan-Air, now at Museum of Flight, East Fortune

This de Havilland DH.106 Comet C.Mk 4 was the final RAF Comet and was one of the last production Comets - actually being the sixth from last built. She made her first flight on March 20, 1962 and was delivered to the Royal Air Force as XR399 on April 26, 1962.

She is seen here as she was in the late 1960s, with her undersides re-painted in light grey to help protect against corrosion, and with minor alterations to the colour scheme, including cheatlines and black 'nose caps' on the pinion tanks, and with 'ROYAL AIR FORCE AIR SUPPORT COMMAND' titles applied above the cheatline. These appeared after the disbandment of Transport Command and the formation of Air Support Command as its successor on August 1, 1967.

The RAF Comets were usually fitted with 94 aft-facing seats, though alternative interior fits could quickly be installed, including dedicated aeromedical and VIP interiors. XR399 flew her fair share of Royal Flights, which included bringing back Prince Charles, Princess Anne, Princess Marina, and Prince Michael together with Earl Mountbatten from a royal wedding in Greece in September, 1964.

The Comet 4s changed their livery again after Air Support Command was absorbed into Strike Command on September 1, 1972, with titles reduced to 'ROYAL AIR FORCE'.

XR399 flew her last RAF sortie on June 25, 1975, and was flown to RAF Leconfield on June 27, formally leaving the fleet on August 29, 1975. When XR399 was retired from RAF service in 1975, she was sold to Dan-Air London and registered as G-BDIX. As G-BDIX the aircraft flew her last service on October 17, 1980 and was flown to Lasham for storage and possible resale on October 29, 1980. Dan-Air ceased Comet services on November 3, 1980.

The aircraft was purchased by the Royal Museum of Scotland (National Museum of Flight) and flown to East Fortune on September 30, 1981, becoming the last Comet to fly in commercial colours. She remains on display to this day, one of East Fortune's most popular exhibits.

BELOW: **The titles on RAF Comet C.Mk 4s changed from 'ROYAL AIR FORCE TRANSPORT COMMAND' to 'ROYAL AIR FORCE AIR SUPPORT COMMAND' in 1967, and finally to 'ROYAL AIR FORCE' in 1972. XR399 was the fifth and final Comet C.Mk 4.** (Malcolm Nason)

Cold War Snoopers

From 1958 to 1974, the Comet performed a vital but secretive role – gathering Signals Intelligence (SIGINT) from around the peripheries of the USSR and its Cold War allies.

RIGHT: **192** Squadron's first Comet, XX663, had a short life - flying the squadron's first operational Comet sortie along the East German border on February 3, 1958 before being lost in a hangar fire on June 3, 1959.

BELOW: **XK659** seen at a snowy Prestwick in 1962, probably for a 'Claret' mission targeting the emissions of a passing Soviet warship. Lossiemouth and Kinloss were the unit's usual Scottish jumping-off points. The 'farting goose' badge on the tail was the work of a squadron pilot, Flight Lieutenant Dave Waltham. (Jim Cain)

Even as the Boeing Washington entered service with 192 Squadron in early 1953, it was realised that the ageing converted bomber was too slow and too vulnerable for the SIGINT role. The Washington lacked the internal volume required to carry sufficient role equipment and operators, and increasing reliance was placed on the squadron's Canberras. The long term plan was to replace both Washington and Canberra with a SIGINT version of the Vickers V1000, but this was unlikely to be in service before 1958. The Avon-engined Comet 2 started to be seen as a potential interim solution. The Comet promised to be able to operate at altitudes of more than 40,000ft, while carrying nine Special Operators and two supervisors.

It was recommended that the RAF should acquire three Comet 2s, with two Ghost-engined Comet 1s as short-term gap-fillers, together with four Avro Shackletons for low level operations. Budgetary pressures led to the approval of a single Comet in August 1954, and in February 1955 the proposed quartet of Shackletons was cancelled and approval was given for two further Comets.

At broadly the same time, the Vickers V1000 was also cancelled, leaving the Comet as more than merely an interim aircraft. The Comet/Canberra pairing was now seen as the way forward, and it was decided that three Comet 2Rs would be augmented by up to four 'operational' Canberras, though the unit would later take further Comets, Canberras, Varsities and Hastings as support aircraft.

With a need for multiple antenna apertures in the pressure cabin, there seemed to be little need to incorporate oval windows. The decision was therefore taken to base the Comet SIGINT conversions on existing BOAC Comet 2s, retaining their square windows.

The decision was taken that the SIGINT Comets would operate to a lower pressure differential (maintaining 4psi rather than 8psi) with the crew wearing oxygen masks.

The aircraft were initially limited to an operational life of just 2,000 flying hours.

The aircraft were modified by Marshall of Cambridge receiving equipment racks, antennas, and other fittings, before having their specialised SIGINT role equipment installed at Watton. There was nearly a ton and a half of this, and SRIM 2113 (the ELINT equipment installation) was described as the 'largest radio modification attempted in any aircraft in the Royal Air Force'.

CREW

The Comet 2R was operated by a flight deck crew of six, with two pilots, a flight engineer, a signaller, and two navigators. The mission crew initially consisted of six Spec Ops (Special Operators) tasked with radar intercept and direction finding (D/F) or ELINT (electronic intelligence), two communications intelligence (COMINT) operators, and two supervisors. The ELINT operators were divided into two three-man teams, one responsible for S-, C- and X-band, and the other for L- and P-Band. Provision was

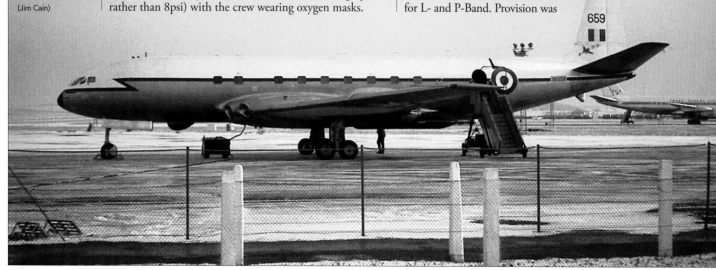

made for three additional Spec Ops to operate the planned 'Breton' equipment when it became available, and, since each of the 13 equipment racks could actually accommodate a pair of operators (for training or relief crew) up to 26 personnel could be carried.

Finding and training Special Operators was a major task, since the Washingtons had carried only six, where the Comets would carry 10, 12 or even 13. Pilots were, surprisingly, not taken from the newly-formed Comet transport unit, 216 Squadron. Instead, Canberra pilots were recruited from Bomber Command, and then underwent a brief Comet conversion course at Lyneham.

Externally, the aircraft carried pencil-like Blue Shadow doppler antennas on the lower 'corners' of the forward fuselage. These flanked the 'teardrop' radome covering the most forward located rotating D/F antenna or 'spinner'. Three more D/F antennas were carried in a ventral canoe further aft. There were further antennas in the nose and tail, and in a cabin window, and there was a plethora of whip antennas and wire aerials on the fuselage top.

The first Comet 2R (XK663) converted by Marshall at Cambridge was flown from Hatfield to Watton for equipment installation on April 17, 1957. The aircraft emerged from installation in July, and then underwent ground tests, minor modifications and calibration flying, becoming operational in December. XK657 was delivered to Watton on July 11, 1957, and entered installation flight in August, emerging in November with a slightly revised equipment fit. XK663 flew 192 Squadron's first operational Comet sortie along the East German border on February 3, 1958, and missions in the Barents Sea, the Baltic, and along the coastlines of Syria, Israel and Egypt soon followed. Missions were usually flown in conjunction with one or two Canberras.

The third Comet, XK655, was delivered to Watton on March 24, 1958, receiving a partial (S-band) Breton installation and new 'spinners', receivers, and analysers. This was known as the Phase 1 1/2 fit, and was completed at the end of August, allowing the aircraft to make its first operational sortie at the beginning of February 1959. By then, 192 Squadron had been re-numbered as 51 Squadron (on August 21, 1958).

The re-numbered squadron's time with three Comets was brief, however, as XK663 burned out after catching fire while undergoing modification work. Brief consideration was given to replacing the aircraft with a VC10, but the cost was prohibitive, and the RAF was unable to reach agreement with BOAC for the purchase of Comet 2E G-AMXK. There were also concerns as to the likely lifespan of the Comet 2Rs, and 51 Squadron was forced to struggle on with two aircraft.

Fortunately, during the first quarter of 1961, tests by the Ministry of Aviation showed that, because they had been operated at such a reduced cabin pressure, the life of

the Comet 2R was (with a couple of minor modifications) likely to be 'almost indefinite'.

It was therefore decided to transfer one of the Transport Command Comet C.Mk 2s, XK695. The plan was strongly supported by GCHQ, which believed that the results from what were euphemistically called 'Radio Proving Flights' were of unique value, and that three Comets was the 'minimum with which an effective programme could be carried out'.

XK695 was modified to an improved standard, by comparison to the original three Comet 2Rs, with more D/F 'spinners' in a second canoe that replaced the forward 'teardrop', and with new receivers, analysers, and recorders. The aircraft was finally delivered to 51 Squadron on September 30, 1963.

The 51 Squadron Comets used a number of different designations, including Comet 2R, C.Mk 2 (RC), C.Mk 2 (RCM), and R.Mk 2. The Comets flew 'Border Sorties' along the so-called Inner German Border, and flew into the Baltic, the Black Sea, the Caspian, and the Barents Sea (the latter using Bodo in Norway as a stepping off point), and mounted sorties against Syria, Israel, and Egypt from Nicosia in Cyprus. Most operations were initially flown on moonless nights, though daylight sorties were flown over West Germany and in the Mediterranean.

MISSIONS

There were three main classes of mission, each with a different designation. AMOs (Air Ministry Operations) were tasked by the Air Ministry and seem to have mainly been concerned with compiling/updating an electronic order of battle in Eastern Europe or the Middle East. The RPF (Radio Proving Flights) designation probably reflected a different tasking authority (e.g., GCHQ). Some operations were noted as DCIs or DCOs (Defence Council Instructions or Operations).

ABOVE: XK655 originally operated with silver-painted undersides, including a silver-painted tailfin, and had a small teardrop radome under the forward fuselage. A small representation of the unit's red goose badge is visible behind the cockpit.

BELOW: Dated May 17, 1961, this photo shows XK655 in the short-lived Signals Command livery that was applied in error after a 'major' overhaul. The aircraft was used as the backdrop of a squadron photo before being sent back for a re-paint!

LEFT: On November 12, 1962, Comet XK659, captained by Wing Commander Cooke, flew to RAF Khormaksar for Operation *Flame*, with Canberra WT305. The series of sorties was targeting a Russian radar supplied to rebel forces by Egypt's Colonel Nasser. (Ray Deacon)

The Squadron also flew so-called Operation *Claret* missions against Soviet warships. Sorties of all types were flown from a number of bases, including Luqa in Malta, Nicosia, and Akrotiri in Cyprus, El Adem and Idris in Libya, Sharjah in the Trucial Oman States, Teheran in Iran, as well as Bodo and Andoya in Norway.

Sharjah started to be used as a base for 51 Squadron's operations in 1962, and in 1963, operations began in the Far East.

Most operations were flown in conjunction with Canberras, with the smaller aircraft often flying feints against the enemy border, to provoke a reaction from the enemy defences that could then be monitored by the Comet crew. "The idea was to 'intimidate' the Soviet defences into coming up to their 'angry' war mode," one former 51 Squadron Spec Op explained. "Fighter AI could be heard to go from track to acquisition and finally lock on. Ground defences were assessed by flying low under radar coverage and then 'popping up' at the last minute in order to trigger the fire control radar."

After a USAF RB-47H was shot down over the Barents Sea on July 1, 1960, 51 Squadron found itself limited to flying no closer than 30nm from enemy coasts or borders, and sudden deviations in track towards enemy territory were briefly banned!

The Comets were regularly upgraded with new mission equipment. Eventually XK655 and XK659 were brought up to virtually the same standard as the 'new' XK695, '655 with the extended forward 'canoe', and '659 without.

The seemingly modest fleet of four Canberras and three Comets operated by 51 Squadron was actually NATO's second-largest airborne SIGINT force and provided NATO's only low level ELINT capability. 51 Squadron's activities were carefully co-ordinated with USAF and US Navy SIGINT missions, and joint operations were even flown on occasion. The squadron earned the respect of the wider SIGINT community for the quality of the intelligence it produced, which was based on the long-serving Special Operators, who often spent decades on the squadron, and whose skill at manipulating their manually tuned receivers was unmatched.

The USAF tended to use wide bandwidth receivers and recorded signals for individual analysis back on the ground. By contrast, 51 Squadron ensured that every one of the signals it intercepted was recognised and located. Because of this philosophy 51 Squadron was responsible for intercepting most of the 'new' signals from which ORBATS were compiled and updated.

BELOW: XK655 is seen here landing at Hatfield in 1973, about a year before her retirement. The aircraft is in the later configuration with a lengthened forward 'canoe' and a revised antenna fit. (Philip J Birtles)

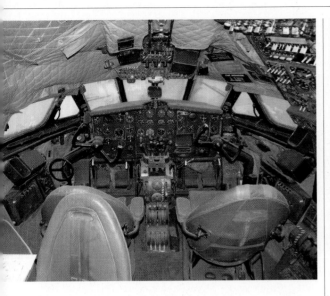

As a result, the Comets and Canberras achieved results that the USAF RB-47s could not. "Quite often we would be tasked to investigate something that the Americans had picked up but couldn't D/F. They'd only know roughly where they'd encountered a particular signal, and whether it was right or left of their track at the time. We'd go and look for it and pinpoint its position more accurately."

The Squadron's aircraft were frequently intercepted by hostile fighters, and occasionally fired upon, but superb navigation and early warnings from the COMINT operators meant that no aircraft were lost. The Comet navigators would never use ground based beacons/aids (which could be 'meaconed') but became very adept at taking star shots and using the on-board Green Satin and Blue Shadow equipment.

The effectiveness of 51 Squadron led to an unprecedented sharing agreement between the US and the UK. Other nations received end-product intelligence analyses derived from SIGINT, whereas the UK received more sensitive raw ELINT data.

A replacement plan for the Comet and Canberra was agreed in 1968, with the Comets rapidly approaching the end of their fatigue lives. Comet operations wound down in 1973, as one crew was removed from operations in order to convert to the Nimrod.

51 Squadron received its first Nimrod R.Mk 1 in February 1974, and flew its first operational Nimrod sortie on May 3, 1974, allowing the retirement of the Comets and Canberras.

RESTAURANT RETIREMENT

XK659 was taken off charge on April 8, 1974 and made her final flight to Manchester on May 13, 1974 having reached the end of her fatigue life. She was dismantled and moved to Pomona Dock where she was reassembled

and became a restaurant annexe for the *North Westward Ho* – Manchester's first 'pub-on-a-ship'. The ship was a former Isle of Wight passenger ferry decommissioned after an explosion in the engine room in 1971. The Comet didn't last long, being scrapped in 1981.

XK655 was the next to go, flying her last operational sortie on July 1 – coincidentally the day that the squadron's Canberra's were withdrawn (though one would return in 1976). She made her final flight to the Strathallan Collection at Auchterarder, Perthshire on August 21, 1974, her undercarriage collapsing on arrival! The museum finally closed in September 1988, but '655 lingered on until she was scrapped in 1990. The nose was saved, and Tim Moore of Skysport Engineering Ltd in Bedfordshire eventually restored it and put it on the roof at Gatwick Airport in 1995, repainted in BOAC colours. This remnant was displayed at Gatwick Airport before moving to the Al Mahattah museum at Sharjah in the UAE in March 2008.

The last Comet (XK695) completed the last home-based Comet series (Operation Minor) on November 14, 1974 and made the final overseas deployment (to Teheran for Operation *Telson*) in December, flying the final sortie in the series (Telson 17) from Akrotiri on December 16, and returning to Wyton on December 18. Two of the crew, flight engineers Bill Cash and Dave Chatten, had been on the first Comet 2R mission on April 17, 1957. The squadron subsequently flew XK695 to the Imperial War Museum at Duxford on 10 January, 1975. Despite being in the care of a national museum, the aircraft had to be broken up in October 1992 because of 'excessive corrosion'. The fuselage went to RAF Newton, where it was used as a training aid for police dogs, until it was scrapped. The nose and front fuselage section was donated to the Mosquito Aircraft Museum in 1995, by Hanningfield Metals in Essex.

ABOVE LEFT: The cockpit of XK655 after her retirement to the Al Mahatta museum in Sharjah, still representative of her time with 51 Squadron, slightly tatty but serviceable! (Rob Feeley)

ABOVE RIGHT: The nose of XK655 is displayed in the Al Mahatta museum in Sharjah, restored in full BOAC markings, with access provided by a set of period airline steps! (Alan Wilson)

BELOW: Supposedly suffering from 'excessive corrosion', XK695 had to be broken up in October 1992 – a poor reflection on the standard of care lavished on this important aircraft by the Imperial War Museum. (Richard Crockett)

de Havilland DH.106 Comet 2R
Comet R.Mk 2, XK655, 51 Squadron

c/n 06023, **Fate:** Retired August 1974, scrapped 1990. Nose survives in Sharjah museum

XK655 served with 51 Squadron from August 21, 1958 to August 1, 1974, the third aircraft for 192 Squadron. The aircraft arrived at Watton on March 24, 1958, following XK663 and XK659. She finally emerged from Installation Flight at the end of August, just as 192 was re-designated as 51 Squadron, with a partial fit of the new Breton SIGINT suite.

51 Squadron's Comets wore a similar colour scheme to the transport Comet C.Mk 2s of Transport Command, albeit with silver-painted undersides rather than highly polished 'natural metal'. By the end of their service, silver had given way to 'light aircraft grey'.

51 Squadron's Comets were kept deliberately anonymous looking, and every effort was made to obscure their role, and to look like 216 Squadron's transport Comets. Thus, in 1960, when this aircraft returned to the unit after maintenance, with Signals Command titles and a black and yellow cheat line, it was immediately realised that the colour scheme would be a bit of a giveaway if the aircraft were intercepted close to the peripheries of the USSR. The aircraft was therefore quickly sent back for a repaint to make it look more like one of 216 Squadron's aircraft!

The aircraft underwent a major upgrade between May 1965 and October 1967, emerging with the later, longer ventral canoe. The in-depth strip down required revealed that while cabin life was almost indefinite, wing fatigue and corrosion meant that the three Comets would have to be withdrawn in about mid-1972, mid-1973 and 1976.

XK655 was the second of 51 Squadron's Comets to be retired, flying a 'working transit' from Luqa to Wyton on July 1, 1974. She was sold to the Strathallan Aircraft Collection and was flown to the Perth-based museum on August 21, 1974. The aircraft hit a hidden obstruction on landing, leading to the collapse of the undercarriage, but she was repaired and put on display. The aircraft was broken up at Strathallan in July 1990. The nose was saved, moving to Lutterworth, Carlisle, Maryport and Hatch, before ending up in Gatwick's spectators' area in 1996. Finally, in March 2008, the nose was shipped to Sharjah's Al Mahattah museum.

BELOW: **XK655 seen resting between sorties from Sharjah in 1962, where she was photographed by a young officer from the Trucial Oman Scouts. The Dave Waltham-designed 'farting goose' badge is visible on the tailfin.** (Peter Aitkens)

de Havilland DH.106 Comet 2R
Comet R.Mk 2, XK659, 51 Squadron

c/n 06025, **Fate:** Retired May 1974, scrapped 1981 after serving as a restaurant

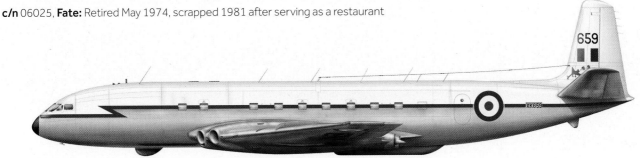

This SIGINT Comet wears an unofficial cartoon version of 51 Squadron's red goose badge - briefly applied to at least two of the squadron's Comets in 1962. The motif was applied sometime after the official red goose behind the cockpit was removed, almost certainly after command of 51 had gone from Derek Rake to 'Chick' Sparrow. The 'farting goose' was designed and applied by one of the squadron's Canberra pilots, Flight Lieutenant Dave Waltham.

On one occasion, during a Comet flight over the Baltic, a Russian Yak-25 'Firebar' pilot gave his controllers the best and most detailed description the linguists on the Comet had ever heard. After flying on one side of the aircraft, he went over the top of the Comet and examined the other side, and then went underneath. He described the aircraft in detail to his controller, going through all of the antennas and radomes, and detailing the markings. He concluded by describing the Comet as an "RAF electronic intelligence-gathering aircraft with 659 on the tail," finishing with the observation that there was a "farting duck painted on each side of the tail fin!"

The equipment fit of 51 Squadron's Comets changed markedly over time, and this was sometimes accompanied by a change to the external antenna configuration. A long ventral canoe was fitted to XK695 when it joined the squadron, later replacing the forward ventral 'teardrop' fairing on XK659. This contained more direction finding 'spinner' antennas.

XK659, was originally built for BOAC but was not delivered to the airline. The aircraft was converted to Comet 2R standards by Marshall in June 1955 and was flown to Watton for equipment installation before being delivered to 192 Sqn on July 20, 1957. 192 Squadron was re-designated as 51 Squadron on August 21, 1958 and moved to Wyton in March 1961. The aircraft was withdrawn from use on May 13, 1974, subsequently becoming the *North-Westward Ho!* bar and restaurant next to the Manchester Ship Canal at Pomona Dock. She was scrapped in October 1981.

BELOW: **XK659 is seen here landing at RAF Luqa on the island of Malta. The long, black, pencil-like antennas below the forward fuselage served the Blue Shadow doppler – used for supporting the aircraft's two navigators and capable of getting a good picture of features such as coastlines and rivers.**

Finale

The mainline airline career of the Comet drew to a close in the early 1970s, but the type continued in military, charter, and experimental use, the last example retiring in 1997.

RIGHT: **More Comets ended their lives being scrapped at Lasham than by any other means! Here a pair of ex-EgyptAir Comet 4Cs wait their fate.** (Alan Pratt)

The Comet 4 disappeared from mainline airlines with astonishing rapidity, as airline after airline withdrew the type in favour of bigger and more modern aircraft. Sudan Airways flew the last scheduled Comet service into Heathrow in 1972, before retiring its two Comet 4Cs in November that year.

That left EgyptAir as the final scheduled airline operating the type, with four aircraft routing to European, Mediterranean and MENA destinations. The Comet 4Cs were retired from June 1975, with SU-AMV operating the last revenue service on May 25, 1976.

In doing so, EgyptAir had outlasted most of the charter and IT airlines operating Comet 4Bs, with Channel Airways having been halted by bankruptcy in February 1972, and BEA Airtours flying its last service on October 31, 1973. Even the RAF's final five Comet C.Mk 4s had been retired to No.60 MU at Leconfield in July 1975!

Both of the Sudan Airways aircraft, all four of the final EgyptAir quartet, five Comet 4Bs from Channel Airways and ten from BEA Airtours were ferried to Lasham where some of them (ten of the Comet 4Bs and one of the Sudan Airways Comet 4Cs) joined Dan-Air, and the remainder were stripped for spares. They were closely followed by the RAF C.Mk 4s.

Dan-Air had become the first British charter airline to buy jet aircraft for IT work when it purchased the first of seven Comet 4s from BOAC in May 1966. Though the Comet burned twice as much fuel as more modern jets, the purchase price was low, and the aircraft combined long range with excellent airfield performance, allowing it to use regional airports and to reach new 'winter market' destinations such as the Canaries.

Dan-Air augmented its former BOAC aircraft with further Comet 4s, eventually operating 13 of the type (with six more purchased for spares). The company then acquired

12 Comet 4Bs and four Comet 4Cs, and finally, in 1975, five ex-RAF Comet C.Mk 4s.

Dan-Air bought a total of 49 Comets, 34 of which flew for the airline, and 15 of which were stripped for spares without ever being flown. The operator never used more than about 20 aircraft at any one time, and the number progressively declined after 1975, as rising oil prices started to bite. There were 14 aircraft in service for the 1978 season, six of them Comet 4Bs, with three 4Cs and five ex-RAF C.Mk 4s. Just seven Comets flew the 1979 season (one 4B, one 4C and five C.Mk 4s) and four C.Mk 4s flew services during the 1980 season.

Dan-Air flew the last Comet 4 commercial service on November 13, 1973, before retiring the aircraft concerned, G-APDB, to the IWM at Duxford on February 12, 1974. The last Comet 4B service was flown by G-APYD on October 23, 1979, and the aircraft was then retired to the Science Museum's out-station at Wroughton.

BELOW: **Perhaps fittingly, it was Dan-Air who brought the Comet's airline career to an end, former RAF Comet C.Mk 4 G-BDIW making the last commercial flight on November 9, 1980. Sister aircraft G-BDIT is seen here in July 1979, on approach to Munich.** (Stefan Rihrich)

The last 'civilian' Comet 4C, G-BDIF, flew its final revenue-earning flight on November 5, 1979, and the final Comet commercial flight was flown by former C.Mk 4 G-BDIW on November 9, 1980, the aircraft then being retired to Düsseldorf on February 7, 1981. The last Dan-Air Comet flight was made on September 30, 1981, with the delivery of G-BDIX to the Scottish National Museum of Flight at East Fortune.

By then, the 'Comwacs' Comet 4, XW626, had retired, flying her last sortie on August 28, 1981.

This left a pair of MOD (Procurement Executive) Comets – XV814 at Farnborough with the RAE and XS235 at Boscombe Down with the Aeroplane and Armament Experimental Establishment. These were destined to be the world's longest-serving Comets, as well as the last.

XV814 was purchased for the RAE's Radio & Avionics Department in January 1967, after serving with BOAC. Following conversion at Chester, and after installation of a removeable under-belly SLIS (Sideways Looking Intercept System) by Marshalls, the aircraft finally entered service in January 1971. A Nimrod-type fin fillet was fitted in June 1971 to cure severe yawing problems, and in early 1972 a new wingtip-mounted pitot system was fitted.

The airframe was used to conduct a range of flight trials from Farnborough including assessments of HF, IR, and magnetometer sensors. Some trials even included real world observation of Soviet defence systems.

The aircraft was painted in the MOD(PE)'s 'raspberry ripple' colour scheme in 1976 and served until December 18, 1992. This ended some 4,850 hours of test and trials flying, with a total of just over 27,000 hours 'on the clock'. The aircraft made its final flight to Boscombe Down on January 28, 1993, where it was used as a spares source for the other surviving Comet, XS235.

Unusually, Comet 4C XS235 was purchased new for the A&AEE and was delivered there on February 12, 1963. She spent her career as a test bed for inertial navigation systems and other equipment, flying all over the world in the process.

During one trial the aircraft even found itself operating in Southeast Asia at the height of the Vietnam war, her

safety ensured by an escort consisting of two USAF F-4 Phantoms!

Canopus made her last operational flight from Boscombe Down on March 14, 1997. On board were John Cunningham (who had flown the very first Comet on its maiden flight) and noted Comet historian Philip Birtles. The aircraft had amassed just 8,281 hours during her 34 year career!

With Comet flying at an end, XV814 was sold for scrap, though the Museum of Flight in Seattle recovered many components for their own ex-Mexicana Comet. The nose was purchased by a private collector, and the tail unit was purchased by BAE Systems for air scoop tests associated with the Nimrod MRA.Mk 4 programme.

The de Havilland Museum Trust bought XS235, but filming work on Steven Spielberg's movie *Saving Private Ryan* prevented the Comet from flying to Hatfield. Instead, she was flown to Bruntingthorpe, where she was gifted to the British Aviation Heritage Collection. She was kept in 'live' condition and regularly taxied. The sale of the bulk of Bruntingthorpe airfield seems to have brought such movement to an end, however.

ABOVE: Farnborough's Comet 4 flying laboratory, XV814, served for more than 12 years after the end of airline operations, finally retiring in January 1993, 20 years after the last Dan-Air Comet 4. She was the penultimate Comet flying. (Chris England)

LEFT: Boscombe Down's *Canopus* (XS235) flew on until 1997, allowing former de Havilland chief test pilot John Cunningham to have been on board both the first and last Comet flights. Boscombe Down resisted all pressure to paint the aircraft in the DERA 'raspberry ripple' colour scheme. (Gordon Bain)

Comet Operators

Considering just 113 Comets ever flew, the type was operated by an impressive number of airlines, holiday companies and military organisations. We take a look at the members of the 'Comet Owners' Club' and those that *nearly* joined.

MAJOR AIRLINES

Aerolineas Argentinas

Loss-making Aerolineas Argentinas made a £9,000,000 commitment to purchase six Comet 4s in 1958, hoping to compete with the jet-equipped US airlines then operating in Latin America, but choosing the Comet because it could operate into airfields that could not accommodate the Boeing 707 or Douglas DC-8.

The first aircraft was officially handed over to the airline on January 28, 1959, and the sixth was delivered in July 1960. Three were lost in accidents, but one replacement Comet 4C was delivered in April 1962. The Comet 4s were relegated to domestic routes from 1966-68, and the four surviving Comet 4s and the 4C were withdrawn and sold to Dan-Air between October and December 1971.

Comet 4: LV-PLM (later LV-AHN), LV-PLO (LV-AHO), LV-PLP (LV-AHP), LV-POY (LV-AHR), LV-POZ (LV-AHS), LV-PPA (LV-AHU),

Comet 4C: LV-PTS (LV-AIB)

Air France

Air France placed an order for three Comet 1As on November 16, 1951, and these were delivered to Le Bourget in June and July 1953. Services began on August 26, 1953, soon after the carrier had ordered three Comet 2s. Three more Comet 2s were ordered in February 1954, but the Comet 2 order was cancelled after the loss of

G-ALYY and the subsequent grounding. Six Comet 2s were laid down for Air France, c/ns 06063-06068.

Comet 1A: F-BGNX, F-BGNY, F-BGNZ

British European Airways (BEA)

BEA placed a £7,000,000 order for six Comet 4Bs in 1957, signing the agreement in March 1959. The first aircraft (G-APMB and G-APMC) were delivered to London Airport on November 16, 1959. Within two weeks of delivery, proving flights had begun to European destinations, but revenue-earning flights only began after April 1960 due to a dispute with pilots over pay and working hours. BEA's first scheduled Comet 4B flight, on April 1, 1960, was unusual in that it was flown not from London but from Tel Aviv. Two other Comet 4Bs were used to begin London-Moscow and London-Nice services.

A seventh aircraft was ordered in August 1959, followed by three more in July 1960. Later that year, in November 1960, a further four Comet 4Bs were ordered. By the middle of 1961 BEA had 14 of the type in service.

A fatal take off accident at Ankara in December 1961 was not sufficient to dent public confidence, and the route network continued to grow. BEA even took the loss of a second aircraft to a terrorist bomb in 1967 in its stride, but scheduled services ended in June 1969.

Two aircraft were retained as back-ups for the airline's new Tridents, and three Airtours Comets were leased back for the same task. Four ex-Olympic Airways Comets were purchased in 1969-1970 before their onward sale.

BELOW: **A Comet 4, LV-PLM, of Aerolineas Argentinas.**

ABOVE: **This Comet 4B, G-APMF, wears the original 1960s BEA 'Red Square' livery.** (Graham Dives)

The BEA Comets were transferred to its subsidiary BEA Airtours in early 1970 with the exception of G-APMA. The latter was scrapped in 1972.

Comet 4C: G-APMA, G-APMB, G-APMC, G-APMF, G-APMD, G-APME, G-APYC, G-APYD, G-APZM, G-APMG, G-ARDI, G-ARCO, G-ARCP. G-ARJK, G-ARGM, G-ARJL, G-ARLM, G-ARJN

British Overseas Airways Corporation (BOAC)

On January 21, 1947, an Instruction to Proceed was issued by the Ministry of Supply for 14 Comets with a total value of over £6,000,000. BOAC and British South American Airways Corporation were to receive the aircraft, but BSAA was absorbed by BOAC in July 1949 with the result that the initial order was reduced to nine aircraft. The nine Comet 1s were delivered to BOAC between December 31, 1951 and September 30, 1952.

BOAC's purchase of 19 Comet 4s was announced in the House of Commons in March 1955 and the company signed the contract in 1957. G-APDB and G-APDC were the first Comet 4s delivered in September 1958 and the final aircraft, G-APDJ, was delivered on January 1, 1960.

The Comet 4s had a brief career on the North Atlantic, flying their last service on October 16, 1960, but were then pressed into service on routes better suited to their size and take off performance. The Comet 4s eventually flew to 46 cities, in 36 countries, across all six inhabited continents.

Captain Cliff Alabaster, the pilot on the first Comet 1 service to Johannesburg, flew the final BOAC Comet 4 service from Auckland to London on November 23, 1965.

BOAC began to offer selected Comet 4s for sale in 1963 and by December 1969 had sold all but one of its Comets, G-APDT, which had just been returned from its lease to Mexicana.

Comet Prototype - G-ALZK (route-proving only)
Comet 1: G-ALYP, G-ALYR, G-ALYS, G-ALYU, G-ALYV, G-ALYW, G-ALYX, G-ALYY, G-ALYZ
Comet 1A: G-ANAV (cancelled by Canadian Pacific Airways)
Comet 2: G-AMXA (route proving only)
Comet 2E: G-AMXD, G-AMXK (Comet 4 route proving and training only)
Comet 3: G-ANLO
Comet 4: G-APDA, G-APDB, G-APDC, G-APDD, G-APDE, G-APDF, G-APDH, G-APDK, G-APDL, G-APDM, G-APDN, G-APDO, G-APDP. G-APDR, G-APDS, G-APDT, G-APDG, G-APDI, G-APDJ

Canadian Pacific Airways

Canadian Pacific Airways was the first overseas customer of the Comet when they ordered 2 Comet 1As. The first one was delivered on March 2, 1953 but was lost the next day following a fatal ground stall at Karachi, killing all on board. CPA cancelled their order for the remaining Comet 1A and soon afterwards placed an order for three Comet 2s with an option for a fourth. This too was cancelled following the Comet accidents in 1954.

Comet 1A: CF-CUM (became G-ANAV for BOAC), CF-CUN (written off at Karachi)

East African Airways

In August 1958, East African Airways placed an order for two Comet 4s for delivery in July and September 1960. EAA ordered a third aircraft in 1960 which was the 72nd and last Comet 4 to be built.

To add to its route capacity, EAA leased G-APDL from BOAC in 1965, re-registering this Comet as 5Y-ADD. EAA also leased three aircraft (5Y-ALD, 5Y-ALF, 5Y- AMT) from Dan-Air in 1970.

The leased 5Y-AMT flew the last EAA service in February 1971 before all of EAA's Comet 4s were flown to Lasham to be scrapped.

Comet 4: VP-KPJ (5X-AAO), VP-KPK (5H-AAF),
Comet 4C: VP-KRL (5Y-AAA),
Leased Comet 4: 5Y-ADD, 5Y-ALD, 5Y-ALF, 5Y-AMT

Kuwait Airways

In August 1962 Kuwait placed an order for two Comet 4Cs for delivery in 1963 and 1964. 9K-ACA was delivered on January 18, 1963 and 9K-ACE was delivered on February 2, 1964. In 1965 it added an ex-BOAC Comet 4, G-APDG (9K-ACI), to its fleet and also leased two BOAC Comet 4s, G-APDN and G-APDS, for one year.

Kuwait retired the aircraft in 1968, although they were brought back into service later that year and leased to Middle Eastern Airlines. They only served MEA until March 1969 when they were again withdrawn from service and stored at Beirut awaiting sale by Kuwait Airways. Dan-Air acquired the fleet, and they were flown back to the UK in 1970 (9K-ACI) and 1971 (9K-ACA and 9K-ACE).

Comet 4C: 9K-ACA, 9K-ACE
Comet 4: 9K-ACI
Leased Comet 4: G-APDG, G-APDN, G-APDS »

de Havilland Comet

ABOVE: This BEA Comet 4B, G-APMG, is seen in the later BEA 'Speedjack' colour scheme. (Graham Dives)

Malayan Airways (later Malaysian Airways and finally Malaysia-Singapore Airlines)

Malayan Airways leased a BOAC Comet 4 in 1962. In 1963 the company became Malaysian Airways and leased a further two BOAC Comets prior to purchasing five Comet 4s from BOAC in September 1965.

In 1966 the company name changed again, this time to Malaysia-Singapore Airlines and three aircraft were re-registered in Singapore (9V-BAS, 9V-BAT and 9V-BAU). In 1967 the airline had to quickly retire two aircraft due to corrosion and then leased two Comet 4s from BOAC (G-APDP which became 9V-BBH, and G-APDM which became 9V-BBJ).

Malaysia-Singapore Airlines retired all its Comets in 1969 and they were sold to Dan-Air at the end of that year.

Comet 4: 9M-AOA (9V-BAS), 9M-AOB, 9M-AOC (9V-BAT), 9M-AOD, 9M-AOE (9V-BAU)
Leased Comet 4: G-APDH, G-APDM (9V-BBJ), G-APDP (9V-BBH)

Mexicana

Mexicana signed a £14,000,000 deal for three Comet 4Cs in October 1959. In order that the aircraft could be supplied in a timely manner, two Comet 4Bs destined for BEA were selected to become the first two Comet 4Cs for the Mexicana order.

BELOW: This Comet 2 wears the early BOAC livery, with a white tail and a straight cheatline.

In December 1964, Mexicana entered a long-term lease deal with BOAC for a Comet 4, XA-NAB (formerly G-APDT) and purchased another, XA-NAZ (formerly G-APDR).

The leased aircraft was returned to BOAC in 1969 and in 1970 XA-NAP was sold to Channel Airways for spares. US aircraft dealer, Westernair, purchased the three remaining Comets.

Comet 4: XA-NAZ (XA-NAP)
Comet 4C: XA-NAR, XA-NAS, XA-NAT
Leased Comet 4: XA-POW (XA-NAB)

Middle East Airlines (MEA)

In January 1959 MEA placed an order for four Comet 4Cs worth £5,500,000. MEA received the first aircraft the following year with the final one being delivered in March 1961.

The airline had an option on a fifth aircraft, G-AROV, but did not take that up, though the aircraft appeared at the 1961 Farnborough air show in MEA colours before being sold to Aerolineas Argentinas.

MEA leased several Comet 4s including G-APDK and G-APDG from BOAC in 1960 and 1961 and G-APDM (registered OD-AEV) in 1967.

On 28th December 1968 Israeli commandos attacked Beirut Airport and destroyed three of MEA's Comets (OD-ADQ, OD-ADR, OD-ADS). The remaining aircraft, OD-ADT, continued to fly until October 1973 when it was purchased by Dan-Air. It was augmented by two Comet 4Cs (9K-ACA, 9K-ACE) and a Comet 4 (9K-ACI) leased from Kuwait Airways in 1968-1969. The last Comet was flown to Lasham for spares on October 4, 1973.

Comet 4C: OD-ADK (OD-ADR), OD-ADQ, OD-ADS, OD-ADT
Leased Comet 4: 9K-ACI, G-APDA, G-APDL, G-APDM (OD-AEV), G-APDS, G-APDI
Leased Comet 4C: 9K-ACA, 9K-ACE
Chartered Comet 4: G-APDK, G-APDG

Misrair/UAA/Egypt Air

On December 30, 1959, Egypt's Misrair signed a £4,000,000 contract for three Comet 4Cs. The first one, >>

BELOW: **The later BOAC colours included a dark blue tailfin and a cheatline that curved down around the nose.** (Ian Haskell)

ABOVE: **Kuwait Airways** acquired a pair of Comet 4Cs as stop-gaps, pending the delivery of Tridents. (Ken Fielding)

SU-ALC, was delivered in June 1960 and the last one, SU-ANU, in 1964.

Misrair and Syrian Airways merged to form United Arab Airlines (UAA) in 1960, and the new carrier placed an order for two more aircraft in January 1961, a further three in 1962 and a final one (SU-ANI, the last civil Comet built), in February 1964.

In 1969 UAA became EgyptAir and phased the Comets onto domestic routes. In 1976 EgyptAir withdrew all its Comets from service, and they were then purchased by Dan-Air who flew three aircraft to Lasham to be used for spares with the last one, SU-ALL, being stripped for spares and left on the airfield at Cairo for scrapping later.

Comet 4C: SU-ALC, SU-ALD, SU-ALE, SU-ALL, SU-ALM, SU-AMV, SU-ANW, SU-ANC, SU-ANI

Olympic Airways
Olympic Airways signed a contract to purchase two Comet 4Bs on 20th July 1959. This was part of a consortium agreement with BEA to operate and maintain the two aircraft. The first aircraft, G-AYPC, was delivered on April 30, 1960. Olympic leased all its remaining aircraft from BEA.

Olympic retired its Comets towards the end of 1969, returning them to BEA to sell on.

Comet 4B: G-APYC (SX-DAK) 'Queen Frederica', G-APYD (SX-DAL) 'Queen Olga', G-ARJK

BELOW: **Malaysian Airways Comet 4** 9V-BAS seen before the name change to Malaysia-Singapore Airlines.

Leased Comet 4B: G-APZM (SX-DAN), G-ARDI (SX-DAO), G-APMB, G-APMF, G-APME, G-APMG, G-ARGM, G-ARJL, G-ARJM, G-ARJN

Sudan Airways
Sudan Airways purchased two Comets in 1962. ST-AAW joined Sudanese independence celebrations in Khartoum that year, having been diverted from pre-delivery flights. It was returned to Hatfield for the completion of testing and was finally delivered to Sudan Airways in January 1963. ST-AAX was delivered in December 1962.

Sudan Airways retired the Comets from service at the end of 1972. ST-AAW was flown to Teesside in the UK whilst ST-AAX remained in Khartoum. Dan-Air purchased the two Comets in 1975. ST-AAW never entered service and was scrapped, but ST-AAX was re-registered as G-BDIF and remained in service until November 1979, which made it Dan-Air's last serving 'civilian' Comet!

Comet 4C: ST-AAW, ST-AAX

UAT (Union Aéromaritime de Transport)
UAT placed an initial order for two Comet 1As on May 1, 1951 for use on its African routes. It added one more Comet 1A in October of the same year. Comet 2s c/ns 06045, 06061, 06062 were all laid down for UAT, but not taken up.

UAT received F-BGSA on December 17, 1952 with F-BGSB following in February 1953. F-BGSC, the third to be delivered, was written off after it overshot the runway at Dakar. The remaining Comets served until April 1954 and then remained at Le Bourget until they were eventually scrapped.

Comet 1A: F-BGSA, F-BGSB, F-BGSC

CHARTER AIRLINES

AREA Ecuador (Aerovias Ecuatorianas CA)
AREA announced the proposed purchase of two ex-BOAC Comets in March, 1966. The first, G-APDI, was delivered to Quinto in March 1966 where AREA registered the aircraft HC-ALT. In 1967 two other ex-BOAC Comets, G-APDJ and G-APDT, were provisionally ordered by AREA, but this was never finalised, and the aircraft were not delivered.

HC-ALT was in service for several years, mainly being used on services between Quito and Miami. In 1968, the aircraft was impounded at Miami where it became the subject of a legal dispute. The aircraft eventually became derelict and was scrapped in February 1978.

BEA Airtours

Seven of BEA's Comet 4Bs were allocated to Gatwick-based BEA Airtours when the former withdrew them from service in June 1969. BEA Airtours operated IT charter flights to destinations across the Mediterranean, as well as ski-related charters to Germany, Austria, and Switzerland. In the event eight aircraft were transferred to BEA Airtours between March 1 and April 1, 1970. These were followed by another two aircraft in May and August that same year.

As Airtours began to introduce ex-Boeing 707-436s as replacements for its ageing Comet fleet, two Comet 4Bs were sold in 1972 and a further three at the beginning of 1973. The last five Comets were withdrawn from service at the end of the summer season 1973 and were all sold (to Dan-Air) by November 9, 1973. The BEA Airtours' Comets carried more than 7 million passengers over 110 million miles during their three-and-a-half year career.

Comet 4B: G-APMC, G-APMF, G-APMD, G-APME, G-APMG, G-ARCP, G-ARJK, G-ARGM, G-ARJL, G-ARJN.

Central African Airways

The Federation of Rhodesia and Nyasaland, also known as the Central African Federation, covered the states of Southern Rhodesia, Northern Rhodesia, and Nyasaland (today the independent nations of Zimbabwe, Zambia, and Malawi) and Central African Airways (CAA) was the supranational airline corporation that served as the Federation's flag carrier.

Leased BOAC Comets were used to operate 'the Rhodesian', a service between Johannesburg and London. Central African Airways survived the dissolution of the Federation of Rhodesia and Nyasaland on December 31, 1963, operating the most prestigious international services and parenting the new subsidiaries of Air Rhodesia, Zambia Airways and Air Malawi.

CAA was disestablished in 1967, and Air Rhodesia, Zambia Airways, and Air Malawi became independent.

Channel Airways

Channel Airways bought five Comet 4Bs from BEA (1 aircraft) and Olympic (4) in 1970, at a cost of £2,000,000. All the Comets retained their original basic colours whilst in service with Channel Airways and were primarily used to operate IT charters for the Lyons Tours Travel Agency, operating in a 109 seat configuration. They also operated on behalf of Mediterranean Holidays and Trident Holidays.

The ex-BEA aircraft, G-ARDI was retired in September 1971 and flown to Southend. This reduced the fleet to four.

Channel Airways purchased XA-NAP (G-APDR), the ex-BOAC and Mexicana Comet for spares, particularly its Rolls-Royce Avon engines. Flown to Stansted, this aircraft was donated to the fire school one year later.

On February 1, 1972 Channel Airways went into receivership and its remaining Comet 4Bs were sold to Dan-Air in April 1972. They were then refitted at Lasham prior to re-entering service.

Comet 4B: G-APMB, G-APYC, G-APYD, G-APZM, G-ARDI
Comet 4: XA-NAP (G-APDR) (Spares only)

Dan-Air

As the largest Comet operator, Dan-Air ultimately owned over half of the Comet 4s built.

The company purchased its first Comet for charter use from BOAC (G-APDK) in 1966, G-APDO following just a few days later. Dan-Air modified its aircraft with a reinforced cabin floor, local strengthening of the wing front spar top and bottom booms, the rear spar top boom, and some lower wing skinning, to allow them to operate safely with Dan-Air's higher ratio of landings to flying hours.

Dan-Air opened a ground school at Horsham, and installed an ex-BOAC Comet simulator, and based a Comet 4 at Newcastle where she was used for training. Another was based at Berlin's Tegel Airport, from where she flew IT flights to Malaga on behalf of a German tour operator!

Dan-Air added to its fleet by purchasing aircraft, all series 4 variants, from other airlines including BOAC, Malaysia-Singapore Airways, East African, Aerolineas Argentinas and Kuwait Airways.

In 1975 Dan-Air purchased five former RAF Comets which had been better maintained than their civil counterparts and were found to be slightly faster, and more fuel efficient than the civil Comets, with slightly lower running costs. The airline's last Comet acquisition consisted of four EgyptAir Comet 4Cs, all of which were used for spares.

Between 1966 and 1976 Dan-Air had purchased 49 of the 77 Comet 4s manufactured, although 15 of them ≫

BELOW: The original Mexicana livery incorporated twin cheatlines above and below the windows.

never flew for the company, and no more than 15-20 were in use at any one time. The 15 unflown aircraft were used for spares to keep the other Comets flying.

G-APYD flew Dan-Air's last holiday flight on October 23, 1979, and G-BDIW flew the last commercial charter (a one hour trip for enthusiasts from Gatwick) on November 9, 1980.

Comet 4: G-APDB, G-APDC, G-APDD, G-APDE, G-APDG, G-APDJ, G-APDK, G-APDL, G-APDM, G-APDN, G-APDO, G-APDP, G-AZIY

Comet 4 unflown: G-APDA, LV-AHN, LV-AHS, 5H-AAF, 5X-AAO, 5Y-AAA

Comet 4B: G-APMB, G-APMD, G-APME, G-APMF, G-APMG, G-APYC, G-APYD, G-APZM, G-BBUV (G-ARCP), G-ARJK, G-ARJL, G-ARJN

Comet 4B unflown: G-APMC, G-ARDI, G-ARGM

Comet 4C: G-AROV (LV-AIB), G-AYVS (9K-ACE), G-AYWX (9K-ACA), G-BDIF (ST-AAX)

Comet 4C unflown: G-ASDZ (ST-AAW), G-BEEX (SU-ALM), G-BEEY (SU-AMV), G-BEEZ (SU-ANC), OD-ADT, SU-ALL

Comet C.Mk 4: G-BDIT, G-BDIU, G-BDIV, G-BDIW, G-BDIX

AIRLINES LEASING OR CHARTERING COMETS

Air Ceylon

During the early 1960s Air Ceylon chartered at least ten BOAC Comet 4s. Full BOAC markings were retained, with 'AIR CEYLON' titles added in red above the cheatline. Air Ceylon commenced services from Colombo Ratmalana to London Heathrow in 1962 using leased BOAC Comet aircraft.

Comet 4: G-APDA, G-APDD, G-APDF, G-APDK, G-APDM, G-APDN, G-APDP, G-APDS, G-APDT, G-APDJ

Air India

Air India placed an order for two Comet 3s but cancelled it after the Comet 1 accident in 1954. It chartered G-APDO from BOAC on April 5, 1962, but the services to Madras (Chennai), Jakarta and Kuwait ended after little more than a year.

Comet 4: G-APDO

Air Malta

Dan-Air wet-leased a Comet (complete with crew, maintenance, and insurance) to Air Malta in May 1976 for services between Malta and Manchester.

Central African Airways

Central African Airways was the airline of the Federation of Rhodesia and Nyasaland (the Central Africa Federation) and operated weekly Salisbury to London services using wet leased BOAC Comets during the early 1960s.

Cyprus Airways

Cyprus Airways (22% owned by BEA) signed an agreement with BEA to begin Comet services in the region. The Comets were flown by BEA flight crews and manned by Cyprus Airways cabin staff.

The Airline suffered two major Comet accidents. BEA Comet 4B G-ARJM stalled shortly after taking off from Ankara, Turkey. The flight crew, cabin crew and 20 passengers lost their lives The second incident took place in October 1967 when G-ARCO was blown up by a terrorist bomb, also killing all on board. The aircraft crashed into the Mediterranean.

Ghana Airways

Ghana Airways showed some brief interest in buying the Comet 4, before briefly leasing a Comet 4 from BOAC to transport President Nkrumah to New York for a conference in March 1961. BOAC titles and logos were overpainted, and 'GHANA AIRWAYS' (and the airline's badge) were applied above the cheatline, together with a Ghanaian flag on the tailfin, and the name 'OSAGYEFO' (The Redeemer) on the forward part of the cheatline.

Comet 4: G-APDA

Guest Aerovias Mexico SA

In late 1960 it was announced that Aerovias Guest planned to replace their Super Constellations on the Mexico City-Paris route. The airline said that it would use Comet 4Cs which they were to lease from Mexicana. Guest signed a lease agreement with Mexicana for two Comet 4Cs in December 1960. The aircraft retained the Mexicana livery, with 'MEXICANA' and 'GUEST' titles added above the cheatline.

Pilots from de Havilland were called on to train Guest crews alongside Mexicana staff. Route proving and training flights began between Mexico City and Paris in April 1961 returning via Lisbon. The two Comet 4Cs used for these flights were XA-NAR and XA-NAT. Scheduled 'Guest' Comet services began in the spring of 1961.

Comet 4C: XA-NAR, XA-NAT

Nigeria Airways

In the mid-60s Nigerian Airways chartered a BOAC Comet to use on its London to Lagos route. The BOAC livery was retained, and the aircraft was operated by BOAC crew.

BELOW: **This Comet 4C wears Middle East Airlines titles in English and Arabic, flanking the shortened MEA.**

Queensland and Northern Territories Aerial Services (QANTAS)

The Chairman of QANTAS, W. Hudson Fysh, was determined not to order the Comet, having experienced some disappointments with other products produced by British manufacturers.

QANTAS did however operate one Comet – G-APDR – which was leased from BOAC for a short period in 1960. It retained the Corporation's markings during the charter. Australia's national airline, QANTAS, operated a joint 'Kangaroo' service with BOAC between London and Sydney during the late 1950s and early 1960s. QANTAS-marked BOAC-operated Comet 4s flew the Sydney-Singapore section of the route. The aircraft retained their basic BOAC livery, albeit with BOAC titles and the 'Speedbird' logo over-painted, and with 'QANTAS' in red above the cheatline and on the pinion tanks. The QANTAS winged kangaroo logo was applied to the tailfin.

Comet 4: G-APDC, G-APDH, G-APDL, G-APDM, G-APDP, G-APDR, G-APDT

South African Airways

South African Airways (SAA) signed an agreement with BOAC in 1953 to establish a joint service between the UK and South Africa. The first service was undertaken on October 4, 1953, crewed by South African Airways employees. A number of aircraft were used, at least some of them wearing a hybrid BOAC/South African Airways livery. G-ANAV, for example, retained full BOAC markings, with a Springbok and South African flag below the registration on the tailfin, mirroring the Speedbird and Union flag, with a Springbok and 'SUID AFRIKAANSE LUGDIENS' on the nose.

Comet 1: G-ANAV, G-ALYY and possibly G-ALYS, G-ALYU, G-ALYW and G-AYLX

Transportes Aereos Portugueses

On June 9, 1959 BEA and Transportes Aereos Portugueses signed a charter agreement to operate a joint service between Madeira and London. Running until 1962, TAP used several Comet 4Bs to run a three times a week service to Lisbon. The aircraft kept their BEA colours, but a small TAP logo was added along the cheat line temporarily blocking BEA's red square logos.

MILITARY and GOVERNMENT OPERATORS

Royal Air Force, 216 Squadron

216 Squadron moved from RAF Fayid in Egypt to RAF Lyneham in November 1955 to allow it to convert to the de Havilland Comet C.Mk 2 jet airliner. With the arrival of the Comet RAF Lyneham's main runway was extended from 6,000 ft to 7,830 ft, necessitating the demolition of two hangars on the north side of the airfield.

The squadron received its first Comet aircraft in June 1956 and began building to a strength of ten Comet C Mk 2s. One aircraft was allocated for conversion to R.Mk 2 standards in 1961, and another went to 51 Squadron as a trainer in 1962, leaving eight C.Mk 2 transports in service. The squadron's Comets operated scheduled services around the world, trooping, carrying VIPs (including the Queen), and conducting casevac operations.

The C.Mk 2s were augmented by five larger Comet C.Mk 4s (based on the civil 4C) from February 1962, and then started to retire from April 1966. The Mk 2s were finally withdrawn in June 1967. The new C.Mk 4 aircraft carried more than twice as many passengers, cruised at a higher speed, and flew further.

The RAF was eviscerated by defence cuts, and with a major reduction in the number of overseas bases, the RAF's transport force was hit particularly hard. 216 Squadron was disbanded on 27 June 1975, after 58 years of service, and its five Comet C.Mk 4s were flown to No.60 MU at Leconfield for disposal.

Comet C.Mk 2: XK669, XK670, XK671, XK695, XK696, XK697, XK698, XK699, XK715, XK716
Comet C.Mk 4: XR395, XR396, XR397, XR398, XR399

Royal Air Force, 192 Squadron, 51 Squadron

The RAF's frontline SIGINT (Signals Intelligence) unit, 192 Squadron, replaced its trio of ageing Boeing Washingtons (B-29 Superfortresses) with the Comet. The Washingtons flew their last sorties (known as 'Radio Proving Flights') in November 1957, and the first Comet, XK663, became operational in February 1958, after some months of calibration and test flying. A second (XK659) started flying operations in April 1958. Like the Washingtons, the Comets were augmented by a flight of English Electric Canberras. »

de Havilland Comet

ABOVE: **Egyptian airline Misrair changed its name to United Arab Airlines, and later EgyptAir.**

The SIGINT aircraft were initially designated Comet 2Rs, but the designations C.Mk 2(RC), C.Mk 2(RCM) and eventually R.Mk 2 were also used.

By the time a third Comet 2R (XK655) was operational, 192 Squadron had been re-designated as 51 Squadron, as part of a wider RAF effort to 'save' older and more historic Squadron 'numberplates'. The Squadron officially became 51 on 21 August 1958 and moved to RAF Wyton in April 1963.

The unit went down to two Comets following the loss of XK663 in a hangar fire in June 1959, with the replacement (a converted C.Mk 2) only reaching the squadron in March 1963.

The unit actually operated as a Special Duties (electronic surveillance) squadron in Signals Command (Bomber Command from 1963, and Strike Command from 1968), though its existence was seldom officially acknowledged, and its role was usually given as calibration or research.

The Comets were replaced by a specialised version of the Nimrod, the R.Mk 1 from 1974, and the final Canberra was retired in 1976.

Comet R.Mk 2: XK655, XK659, XK663, XK695,
Comet C.Mk 2: XK671, XK697, XK715

UK Research and Development

The UK operated a Comet 1A, a Comet 1XB, two Comet 2Es, the sole Comet 3, three Comet 4s and a Comet 4C in a variety of experimental, research, development, and trials roles. These aircraft were operated by a complex network of interlinked units, most of them coming under the auspices of the Royal Aircraft Establishment at Farnborough and Thurleigh (Bedford), the Royal Signals and Radar Establishment at Pershore, and the Aeroplane and Armament Experimental Establishment at Boscombe Down.

These Establishments (and industry operated aircraft) came under the control of the Ministry of Supply until November 1959. Thereafter they came under the Ministry of Aviation until 1967, the Ministry of Technology from 1967-70, the Ministry of Aviation Supply from 1970-71, and finally the Ministry of Defence (Procurement Executive) in 1971.

The last Comets had retired by the time the MoD(PE) was superseded by the Defence Procurement Agency on April 1, 1999, though the A&AEE (renamed the Aircraft and Armament Evaluation Establishment in 1992) became part of the Defence Research Agency and passed from the MoD Procurement Executive to the Defence Test and Evaluation Organisation (DTEO) in 1993, and subsequently to the Defence Evaluation and Research Agency (DERA) in 1995.

The RAE, meanwhile, was renamed the Royal Aerospace Establishment (RAE) in 1988 and merged with other research entities to become part of the new Defence Research Agency in 1991, and on April 1, 1995 the DRA was merged into the Defence Evaluation and Research Agency (DERA).

Comet 1A G-ANAV: MoS/RAE for data gathering flights in support of Comet 1 crash investigation.
Comet 1XB XM823: de Havilland Propellers for IR-guided missile development.
Comet 1XB XM829: A&AEE for high altitude navigation trials including Decca and Dectra.
Comet 2E XN453: RAE Radio Flight for radio, Satcom, jammer and IRCM trials.
Comet 2E XV144: Smiths Instruments, then RAE Blind Landing Experimental Unit.
Comet 3 XP915: RAE Blind Landing Experimental Unit, then MR role profile and wake turbulence research.
Comet 4 XV814: replacement for XN453, plus SIGINT development with 'Kalki' digital SLIS (Sideways Looking Intercept System).
Comet 4 XW626: RSRE Pershore for AEW radar trials, later trial installation for Nimrod AEW.Mk 3 with BAe, RSRE, and RAE Bedford.
Comet 4 XX944: A&AEE. Unknown trials work.
Comet 4C XS235: Built for the A&AEE as a trials aircraft for radio, INS, and other navigation systems. Operated until March 1997, becoming the World's last flying Comet

Royal Canadian Air Force, 412 Squadron

The Royal Canadian Air Force placed an order for two de Havilland Comets in November 1951, aiming to replace lumbering Canadair North Star transports in RCAF Service, but also using the aircraft as high speed 'silent targets' to assess Canada's fighter forces and radar chain.

More than 60 air and ground crew from 412 Squadron were sent to England to receive familiarization training on

the Comet in October 1952, and the RCAF received its first Comet in the UK on 14 March 1953. The two RCAF crews subsequently flew over 100 training hours, including flights to Johannesburg and Singapore. On Friday, May 29, 1953, the first Comet arrived at RCAF Station Uplands in Ottawa, making the RCAF the first air force in the world to operate jet transports and the first operator to make scheduled trans-Atlantic crossings.

The Comets were withdrawn from service in January 1954 after the BOAC Comet 1 crashes. When the cause had been pinpointed, the Comets were ferried to Chester for structural modifications in August 1956. They were returned to service on November 1, 1957 as Mark IXBs. The RCAF Comet flew its last scheduled flight into Marville on March 1, 1962, giving way to the CC-106 (CL-44) Yukon. The Comets continued to operate special services, with the very last flight made on August 8, 1963.

Comet 1A (later 1XB): 5301, 5302

Saudi Royal Flight
The Government of Saudi Arabia ordered a single Comet 4C for the use of King Saud bin Abdul Aziz – Saudi Arabia's second King, who ruled from 1953 to 1964. The Comet 4C was delivered on June 15, 1962, but crashed on the night of March 20, 1963, killing the eight crew members and the ten members of the Saudi Royal Family who were on board at the time.

The aircraft was flying above the Alps and along the border between France and Italy and descended below the cleared height of 10,000 feet given by Air Traffic Control, causing it to fly into the slope of Mt Matto.

Comet 4C: SA-R-7

PROSPECTIVE CUSTOMERS

Air India
An order for two Comet 3s, for delivery in 1957, was cancelled by Air India following the Comet 1 accidents in 1954.

British Commonwealth Pacific Airlines
British Commonwealth Pacific Airlines ordered three Comet 2s for their Sydney to Vancouver route, but the airline was taken over by TEAL in 1954 and the order did not go ahead.

British South American Airways Corporation
The initial 1947 BOAC order for 14 Comets included six aircraft for BSAAC, but the two companies were merged in 1949 and just nine Comets were delivered to BOAC, commencing in December 1951.

Capital Airlines
Capital Airlines, which had pioneered the use of the turboprop Viscount in the US, placed an order for four Comet 4s and ten Comet 4As in July 1956, with a value of around £19,000,000. The Comet 4s were due for delivery in late 1958, with the Comet 4As following from late 1959. »

BELOW: Dan-Air's Comet 4 G-APDJ seen in front of Gatwick's brutalist architecture in June 1970. (Graham Dives)

However, Capital was taken over by United Airlines in 1961 and the order was cancelled. The Comet 4A was never built.

Compania Aeronautica Uruguaya SA (CAUSA)

It was thought that Compania Aeronautica Uruguaya SA was going to buy a BOAC Comet 4 in 1967, but the sale was never completed. The aircraft concerned – G-APDN – was leased to Dan-Air, London in October 1967 and was finally sold to Dan-Air in May 1968.

Dick Drost

Dick Drost purchased one of the three ex-Mexicana/ Westernair Comet 4Cs (and a simulator) for his 'Naked City' nudist colony in Indiana. The aircraft (N999WA) was flown from storage in Albuquerque to Chicago O'Hare. However, it was never used by the colony and was eventually scrapped at Chicago in 1993.

Eastern Airlines

Former Great War fighter ace turned airline boss Eddie Rickenbacker negotiated a deal for more than 30 Comet 3s and several Comet 2s for Eastern Airlines in 1952. Unfortunately, the contract was never ratified.

Japan Air Lines (JAL)

Japan Airlines signed up for a pair of Comet 2s (plus four Herons and four Doves) on November 18, 1952, but the order was cancelled three years later, in the wake of the Comet 1 crashes. Three Comet 2s were laid down at Hatfield for JAL (c/n 06042, 06043 and 06044).

KLM (Royal Dutch Airlines)

KLM's interest in the Comet 3 did not survive the Comet 1 crashes.

LAV (Linea Aerospatial Venezolana)

LAV ordered two Comet 2s in July 1953 for use on the Caracas-New York route. Two aircraft (c/n 06039 and 06040) were under construction when the order was cancelled following the Comet 1 crashes.

Lufthansa

Lufthansa, whose creation was then still being considered by the Gesellschaft für Luftverkehrsbedarf, nearly ended up a Comet operator, evaluating Comet 1 G-ALYY at Köln/ Bonn in April 1953, and considering the Comet 3 for the Frankfurt-New York route. The order was cancelled following the Comet 1 crashes.

Merpati Nusantara Airlines

Merpati Nusantara Airlines was an Indonesian airline based in Central Jakarta. It operated scheduled services to more than 25 destinations in Indonesia and scheduled international services to East Timor and Malaysia. There have been reports that the airline operated a Comet 2 in 1972, but this seems most unlikely.

National Airlines

Miami-based National Airlines announced its intention to purchase 12 Comet 2s and 3s in October 1953. The £12 m order was cancelled following the Comet 1 crashes.

Overseas National Airlines

In late 1951, George Tompkins' Oakland-based Overseas National Airlines reportedly considered ordering two de Havilland DH.106 Comets, but no order materialized, after the US Civil Aeronautics Authority refused to accept British CAA certification of the type.

Pacific Western Airlines

Pacific Western planned to use three Comet 4s to fly Trans-Canada services before abandoning the plan.

Pan American World Airways

Pan Am announced its purchase of three Comet 3s (with options on seven more) in October 1952 – the first order for a British-built airliner for a US airline. The aircraft were due for delivery in 1957, using three of the aircraft that had been earmarked for BOAC. The Comet 1 disasters led to the cancellation of the order.

Panair do Brasil

It was announced that Panair do Brasil was considering a Comet order on April 6, 1951, and a contract for four Comet 2s (with options for further Comet 3s) was signed in February 1953. The order was cancelled following the Comet 1 crashes, but one Comet 2 was laid down at Hatfield for Panair (c/n 06041).

Redmond Air

Redmond Air bought the three ex-Mexicana Comet 4Cs from Westernair, hoping to provide charter flights between Washington State and Las Vegas. N888WA got as far as being delivered to Everett, but never entered service.

Westernair

Westernair purchased three Comet 4Cs from Mexicana in 1973, refurbishing and repainting the aircraft, and hoping to sell them (with spares, ground support equipment and a simulator) as a package. One remained in Mexico, eventually ending up in a children's playground, while two were flown to the USA.

Comet 4C: N777WA, N888WA, N999WA

BELOW: This highly polished Comet C.Mk 2 served with the RAF's 216 Squadron at RAF Lyneham. (Urs Baettig)

What Happened to the Comets?

De Havilland completed and flew 113 Comets, with another airframe being completed and flown as the second Nimrod prototype – the first Nimrod flying one sortie as a Comet 4C and thus being counted in the 113 Aircraft total! There were also a number of static test airframes.

These 113 aircraft included two Comet 1 prototypes, nine Comet 1s, and ten Comet 1As. Four of the latter were subsequently converted to Comet 1XB standards.

There was also one Comet 2X prototype (a hybrid with the Mk 1 Airframe but with Avon engines) and 15 flying Comet 2s. Some 39 Comet 2 construction numbers (c/ns) were allocated to production Comet 2s, but 24 of these were never flown, and many were never completed. Of the 15 fliers, just four ever flew in BOAC markings, and none ever carried a fare-paying passenger. Two of the BOAC Comet 2s were converted to Comet 2E standards before being transferred to experimental duties.

Of the Airworthy Mk 2 Aircraft, ten were completed as C.Mk 2s for the RAF – one after flying first as a Comet 2 destined for BOAC, two initially flying as T.Mk 2s. One C.Mk 2 was later converted to Comet 2R standards. Three were completed as Comet 2Rs (R.Mk 2s) for RAF Signals Command, two of these after making their first flights in civil guise.

The Comet 3 flew only in prototype form, though ten c/ns were allocated.

De Havilland then built 28 Comet 4s (19 for BOAC, six for Aerolineas Argentinas, and three for East African Airways), 18 Comet 4Bs and 23 Comet 4Cs. Three of the Comet 4Cs were built for Mexicana, nine for MisrAir/UAA, four for MEA, two for Sudan Airways, one for Aerolineas Argentinas, two for Kuwait Airways, one for the Saudi Royal Flight and one for the UK MOD.

There were five Comet C.Mk 4s for the RAF, and two unsold and unfinished Comet 4Cs were completed as HS801 Nimrod prototypes.

Of these, two uncompleted Comet 2s were built in Belfast, while Chester built one of the flying Comet 2s (plus four that were not completed and 20 more that

were abandoned or not started). Chester also built 17 Comet 4s, two Comet 4Bs, 16 Comet 4Cs, five Comet C.Mk 4s and the Nimrod prototype Airframes - representing the majority of the Comet 4 family.

The following pages provide some highlights of the individual Aircraft's histories, which are presented in construction number order. For compactness, they are presented in note form, using the abbreviations shown (bottom left).

COMET 1 & 2X

06001, G-ALVG, Comet prototype

FF 27/07/49 as **G-5-1**. D'd MoS 01/09/49 as **G-ALVG**. Fitted with four-wheel main u/c bogeys from Dec 49-Jan 50. Painted in BOAC colours by mid-1951. Last flight 31/07/53. Structural testing at Farnborough until 09/54. Scrapped late 1950s.

06002, G-ALZK, second prototype

FF 27/07/50. D'd MoS 07/50. Loaned to BOAC Comet Unit at Hurn. Wfu 03/57. Then used for ground testing. Scrapped at Woodford mid-1970s.

06003, G-ALYP, Comet 1

FF 09/01/51. D'd to BOAC 13/03/52. World's first scheduled jet service to Johannesburg 02/05/52. Crashed into Mediterranean off Elba following structural failure 10/01/54. All six crew and all 29 passengers killed. Wreckage recovered to Farnborough for investigation and scrapped later in 1954.

06004, G-ALYR, Comet 1

FF 28/07/51. D'd to BOAC 17/05/52. Taxiing accident Calcutta 25/07/53. Cocooned London Airport late 1953, but repairs not actioned. Removed to Farnborough 06/55 and later scrapped.

06005, G-ALYS, Comet 1

FF 08/09/51. D'd to BOAC 04/02/52. D'd Farnborough for testing 24/04/54. Wfu 01/07/55. Believed to have been scrapped at Farnborough c.1961.

06006, G-ALYT, Comet 2X prototype

Prototype for the Comet 2, with Comet 1 fuselage, but powered by Avon 502 engines. FF 16/02/52. D'd to Ministry of Supply 01/03/52. Leased to BOAC for route-proving 29/07/53. Returned 23/09/53. Flown to RAF Halton for ground instructional use 28/05/59. Maintenance serial **7610M**, with code '8'. Engines removed 1966. Scrapped 1967.

06007 G-ALYU, Comet 1

FF 13/12/51. D'd to BOAC 06/03/52. Wfu 09/04/54. Flown to Hatfield next day. Taken by road to RAE Farnborough for water tank tests 07/05/54. Fuselage to Cardiff Airport for passenger escape trials in 1955. Fuselage sections to Stansted Fire School 1961, burned 1962.

06008, G-ALYV, Comet 1

FF 09/04/52. D'd to BOAC 23/04/52. Aircraft broke up in flight in thunder squall near Jugalgari (30 miles from Calcutta) 02/05/53. All six crew and 37 passengers killed. Some wreckage returned Farnborough later in 1953. Rest of wreckage delivered to RAE Farnborough 14/05/54.

06009, G-ALYW, Comet 1

FF 25/02/52. D'd to BOAC 14/06/52. Returned to London Airport 27/04/54. Cocooned London Airport pending wider Comet disaster investigations June 1954. Transported to and then cocooned at RAE Farnborough June 1955. Moved to No.71 MU 1969. Converted to Nimrod travelling exhibit 'XV238', operating company EPTU Serco Ltd.

06010, G-ALYX, Comet 1

FF 09/07/52. D'd to BOAC 23/07/52. Returned to UK after G-ALYP/G-ALYY accidents 21/04/54. Dismantled at Hatfield, moved to Farnborough for possible tests 1955. Fuselage, tail planes, landing gear cocooned at Farnborough 1955. Noseless fuselage to RAE Lasham 1963. Believed scrapped at Lasham 1996.

06011, G-ALYY, Comet 1

FF 10/09/52. D'd BOAC 23/09/52. Lost near Stromboli after inflight structural failure while operating with SAA and w/o 08/04/54. All seven crew and 14 passengers killed.

06012, G-ALYZ, Comet 1

FF 23/09/52. D'd to BOAC 30/09/52. W/o during a take-off accident at Rome Ciampino Airport 26/10/52. No fatalities. Nose used for fire training at Heathrow.

COMET 1A

06013, CF-CUM/G-ANAV, Comet 1A

FF 11/08/52 as **CF-CUM** *Empress of Vancouver*, but never entered service with Canadian Pacific Airlines. Sold to BOAC 12/08/53 and re-reg'd **G-ANAV** 15/08/53. Purchased by RAE/MoS for investigations and research and delivered to Farnborough 03/05/54. Aircraft scrapped Farnborough. Nose sold to Science Museum London 21/05/62. Transferred to Science Museum out station at Wroughton 16/12/94. Donated to the de Havilland Aircraft Museum by the Science Museum in May 2016. **Nose still extant at London Colney in 2022.**

06014, CF-CUN, Comet 1A

FF 24/12/52. D'd to Canadian Pacific Airways as *Empress of Hawaii* 02/03/53. Set off from London for inaugural service from Australia to Hawaii. W/o at Karachi 03/03/53 in the first fatal Comet accident. Stalled on take-off, all 11 on board killed.

06015, F-BGSA, Comet 1A

FF 13/11/52. D'd to UAT France 16/12/52. Flew first UAT service 19/02/53. Wfu 12/04/54. Scrapped Le Bourget 1961.

06016, F-BGSB, Comet 1A

FF 21/01/53. D'd to UAT France 20/02/53. Wfu 12/04/54. Scrapped Le Bourget 1961.

06017, RCAF 5301, Comet 1A, later 1XB

FF 21/02/53. D'd to No.412 Sqn, RCAF, for training at Hatfield 18/03/53. D'd to Uplands Airport, Ottawa 29/05/53, breaking Atlantic Speed Record en route. Wfu April 1954 following loss of G-ALYY. Modified to Comet 1XB standards at Chester during 1957. FF as

1XB 02/08/57 and returned to service. Wfs 03/10/63 and last flight to Mountain View 30/10/63. Scrapped at CFB Mountain View 30/10/65. Nose to National Aviation Museum, Rockcliffe (held in storage) 1965. **Nose still extant at Rockcliffe in 2022.**

06018, RCAF 5302/CF-SVR/N373S, Comet 1A, later 1XB

FF 25/03/53. D'd Royal Canadian Air Force 13/04/53. Wfu 04/54. Returned to Chester for 1XB conversion 25/05/56. Re-d'd to RCAF 26/09/57. Wfu 03/10/63. Flown to Mountain View pending disposal 30/10/63. Sold to Eldon Armstrong 30/07/65 and re-reg'd **CF-SVR**. Sold to Bob Quigley Aircraft Sales 1965. Sold to B Dallas Airmotive July 1967 and re-reg'd **N373S**. Sold to Lisbon Development Company Miami, 1968. Sold to the Aldebaran Company November 1968. Sold to Buddy Reid 1969. Sold to R C Rose February 1970. Scrapped Miami 1975.

06019, F-BGSC, Comet 1A

FF 15/04/53. D'd to UAT France 30/04/53. Crashed at Dakar, Senegal skidding off the runway on landing 25/06/53. Scrapped Dakar Airport after 1954.

06020, F-BGNX/G-AOJT, Comet 1A

FF 06/05/53. D'd to Air France 12/06/53. Wfs 11/01/54 following loss of G-ALYP at Elba. Sold to Ministry of Supply April 1954. Re-reg'd **G-AOJT** 11/05/56. Wfu 09/07/56. Broken up Farnborough August 1956. Moved to fire dump Farnborough 1970. Fuselage remained Farnborough until 1985. Acquired by de Havilland Museum and delivered there 20/03/85. The fuselage of F-BGNX remains on display at the de Havilland Aircraft Museum. **Fuselage still extant at London Colney in 2022.**

06021, F-BGNY/G-AOJU/XM829, Comet 1A, later 1XB

FF 22/05/53. D'd to Air France 07/07/53. Wfs 11/01/54 and converted to Comet 1XB standards at Chester in 1954. Re-reg'd **G-AOJU**. FF from Chester as 1XB 23/09/57. Transferred to military marks as **XM829** 14/10/58. Allocated A&AEE Boscombe Down on a five year loan. Delivered Stansted Fire School 20/02/64. Dumped at Stansted late 60s. Burned autumn 1970 and then scrapped.

06022, F-BGNZ/G-APAS/XM823, Comet 1A, later 1XB

FF 16/03/53. D'd to Air France 22/07/53. Grounded 11/01/54 following G-ALYP accident at Elba. D'd to Hatfield as **G-5-23** 18/02/54. To Chester for Comet 1XB modifications in 1956. Gained strengthened fuselage, elliptical windows, and Ghost 50 engines, 1956. Reg'd to Ministry of Supply as **G-APAS** 23/05/57. FF as 1XB 29/11/57. Serialled **XM823** transferred to de Havilland Propeller Co under MoS contract 10/02/58. D'd 30/01/58. Blue Jay trials. Temporary transfer to English Electric at Warton for Lightning trials May 1958. Painted matt black with dayglo centre section during 1959-60 - probably for Red Top missile trials. De Havilland Propellers became Hawker Siddeley Dynamics at around this time. Re-engined April 1964 using engines from XM829. AJ168 Martel missile datalink trials April 1965. Contract extended in 1965 until 30/04/67. Wfu and SOC 30/11/67. Made last Comet 1 flight 08/04/68 to Shawbury allocated **8351M** (not worn). Transferred to RAF Museum Cosford and restored to BOAC

colours (which it never wore in service!) as **G-APAS** in 1978. Remains on display at the RAF Museum Cosford, the only complete Comet 1 in existence. **Entire aircraft still extant at Cosford in 2022.**

COMET 2

06023, G-AMXA/XK655, Comet 2/2R

FF 27/08/53, delivered to BOAC during latter part of 1953. Wfs April 1954. Reg'd Ministry of Supply 18/03/55. Allocated XK655 13/07/55 and delivered to Marshall of Cambridge for conversion to Comet 2R. Loaned to de Havilland Aircraft Co. for radar trials 18/02/58. To No.192 Sqn, Watton, 24/03/58. No.192 Sqn re-designated as No.51 Sqn 21/08/58. No.51 Sqn to RAF Wyton 31/03/61. Coded 'A' 17/01/71. Wfu 01/08/74. Purchased by Strathallan Museum, Perth 01/08/74. Flown to Strathallan 21/08/74, damaged on landing and repaired. Purchased by Midlands-based scrap dealer July 1990. Nose section sold to Mr F Walker, Carlisle 27/11/90. Sold to Mr D Price, Cockermouth 1992. Moved to Carlisle Airport, May 1994. Gatwick Airport, Skyview Visitor Centre 12/12/95. To Hatch for storage 28/01/04. Nose shipped to Sharjah-Al Mahatta Museum 28/03/08. **Nose still extant at Al Mahatta in 2022.**

06024, G-AMXB/XK669, Comet 2/ T.Mk 2/C.Mk 2

FF 03/11/53, built for BOAC, but not delivered. Reg'n cancelled 02/03/55. Sold to Ministry of Supply 18/03/55. XK669. FF as T.Mk 2 09/12/55. Delivered No.216 Sqn. RAF Lyneham 08/06/56. Converted to C.Mk 2 03/01/58. Returned to No.216 Sqn 23/05/58 and named *Taurus* and eventually wfu 22/04/66. Nose taken to RAE Farnborough 1969. Burnt on fire dump Lyneham 1970.

06025 G-AMXC/XK659, Comet 2/2R

FF 25/11/53, used by BOAC for route-proving without passengers. Reg'n cancelled 02/03/55. Sold to Ministry of Supply 18/03/55. Allocated for 2R modification by Marshall 27/06/55. Allocated **XK659** 13/07/55. FF as Comet 2R 12/07/57. D'd No.192 Sqn, RAF Watton 20/07/57. No.192 Sqn re-designated as No.51 Sqn 21/08/58. No.51 Sqn to RAF Wyton 31/03/61. Coded 'B' 1971. SOC 08/04/74. Sold to Compass Catering Ltd 13/05/74, flown to Manchester Airport on the same day. Moved to Pomona Dock to become 'North-Westward Ho Restaurant and Bar', 10/06/74. Scrapped October 1981. Nose to Mr Michael Runciman, moved to Elland, W.Yorks Jan 1982, scrapped April 1990.

06026, G-AMXD/XN453, Comet 2/2E

FF 20/08/54. Sold to Ministry of Supply 18/03/55. Converted to Comet 2E 1957. D'd to Ministry of Supply 29/08/57, used by BOAC Comet Flight for route proving for Comet 4 29/08/57 to 16/09/57. Sold to RAE Farnborough 15/04/59 as **XN453** (serial from 20/04/59). Fitted with RCM and navaids. Special radio trials. Last flight 09/02/73. To Farnborough dump, burned 1984.

06027, G-AMXE/XK663, Comet 2/2R

Built for BOAC, but reg'n cx 02/03/55. Sold to Ministry of Supply 18/03/55. **XK663**. FF 18/07/55 and converted to 2R by Marshall, FF as 2R 17/04/57. D'd No.192 Sqn RAF Watton 19/04/57. No.192 Sqn re-designated as No.51 Sqn 21/08/58. Burnt out hangar fire at RAF Watton 03/06/59.

06028, G-AMXF/XK670, Comet 2/T.Mk 2/ C.Mk 2

Built for BOAC, but reg'n cancelled 02/03/55. Sold to Ministry of Supply 18/03/55. FF as Comet T.Mk 2 **XK670** 12/03/56. D'd to No.216 Sqn RAF Lyneham 07/06/56. First RAF Comet 'op' to Moscow 23/06/56 for VIP visit to Tushino Air show (also first British jet flight to Moscow). Converted to C.Mk 2 13/11/57. Returned to No.216 Sqn 18/04/58 as *Corvus*. Wfu 08/08/66. Reg'd **7962M** and used for fire rescue training at Lyneham. Burned 1968.

06029, G-AMXG/XK671, Comet 2/C.Mk 2

Built for BOAC, but reg'n cancelled 02/03/55. Sold to Ministry of Supply 18/03/55. FF as C.Mk 2 **XK671** 16/07/56. To A&AEE for handling trials 21/08/56. D'd to No.216 Sqn RAF Lyneham 16/10/56. Named *Aquila* 29/08/58. Transferred to No.51 Sqn at Wyton as trainer/support aircraft 18/09/62, coded 'T'. Wfu (RAF Wyton) 31/03/64. Transferred to No.71 MU for disposal 31/03/64. Last flight to RAF Topcliffe 14/11/66. Instructional Airframe **7927M** until dumped July 1973.

06030, G-AMXH/XK695, Comet 2/C.Mk 2/R.Mk 2

Built for BOAC, but reg'n cancelled 02/03/55. Sold to Ministry of Supply 18/03/55. FF as C.Mk 2 **XK695** 21/08/56. D'd to No.216 Sqn RAF Lyneham 14/09/56. Named *Perseus* 13/11/57. Delivered Marshall for conversion to 2R 31/07/61. Delivered to No.51 Sqn 08/03/63. Coded 'C' 1971. Flown to Duxford to join IWM collection on loan as **9164M** 10/02/75, having completed 8,236 flying hours in over 3,200 flights. Broken up at Duxford, October 1992, due to corrosion in the undercarriage. Fuselage transported to RAF Newton for use by RAF police dog training unit 1992. Sold to Hanningford Metals, Stock, Essex and cut up, but nose retained Sept 1995. Hanningford Metals donated nose to de Havilland Aircraft Museum, London Colney, 17/12/95. **Nose still extant at London Colney in 2022.**

06031, G-AMXI/XK696, Comet 2/C.Mk 2

Built for BOAC, but reg'n cancelled 02/03/55. Sold to Ministry of Supply 18/03/55. FF as C.MK 2 **XK696** 29/09/56. D'd to No.216 Sqn RAF Lyneham 14/11/56. Named *Orion* 21/03/57. Transported to RAF Watton late 1966. Used for trial equipment fit for No.51 Sqn. Scrapped Watton Nov 1969.

06032, G-AMXJ/XK697, Comet 2/C.Mk 2

Built for BOAC, but reg'n cancelled 02/03/55. Sold to Ministry of Supply 18/03/55. FF as C.Mk 2 **XK697** 17/11/56. D'd to No.216 Sqn RAF Lyneham 12/12/56. Named *Cygnus* 08/08/57. Wfs 01/03/67. Transferred to No.51 Sqn, RAF Wyton 01/03/67, coded 'D'. Wfu 09/02/73. Donated to local Air Scouts as HQ 20/12/73. Declared unsafe in 1987 and broken up.

06033, G-AMXK/XV144, Comet 2/2E

Conv'd Comet 2E and FF 10/07/57. D'd to BOAC 26/08/57 and used for route-proving trials September 1957 to January 1958. Sold by BOAC to Ministry of Aviation 21/01/60. Used by Smiths Autoland and Smiths Industries at Hatfield. Allocated to RAE 02/09/65. D'd to RAE Bedford (for BLEU) 11/18/66 with new serial **XV144**. Flown Farnborough for spares recovery 16/06/71. Scrapped by J S Shackleton at Siddal August 1975.

06034, G-AMXL/XK698, Comet 2/C.Mk 2

Built for BOAC, but reg'n cancelled 02/03/55. Sold to Ministry of Supply 18/03/55. FF as C.Mk 2 **XK698** 13/12/56. D'd to No.216 Sqn RAF Lyneham

10/01/57. Named *Pegasus* 08/02/58. Wfs 09/06/67. Transferred to No.27 MU Shawbury 09/06/67. Re-serialled **8031M** 13/09/68. Moved to No.19 MU St Athan and broken up April 1973.

06035, XK699, Comet C.Mk 2

Built for BOAC and nominated to become Comet 2R (not taken up) 17/03/55. Sold to Ministry of Supply 18/03/55. FF as C.Mk 2 **XK699** 02/02/57. D'd to No.216 Sqn RAF Lyneham 20/02/57. Named *Sagittarius*. Wfu April 1967. Retired to RAF Henlow, last flight 13/06/67. Re-serialled **7971M** 14/06/67. Gate Guardian RAF Lyneham d'd 17/10/86. Destined for RAF Museum Cosford in Shropshire after the Ministry of Defence closed RAF Lyneham, but the tender to dismantle and relocate the jet was cancelled in 2012 as the level of corrosion in the fuselage would have made this too expensive. Airframe scrapped 11/13, front fuselage saved for Old Sarum Museum. Boscombe Down Aviation Collection (BDAC) used the scrap value of the back end of the Aircraft to fund the dismantling and removal of the front end of the Comet. **Nose still extant at Old Sarum in 2022.**

06036, Comet 2, prototype/trial installation for RAF configuration

Work halted on Airframe April 1954. Allocated as the Transport Command prototype 17/03/55. Then finished to C.Mk 2 standard and completed with RAF colour scheme. Placed in water tank at Hatfield for fatigue life structural testing 1956. Removed from tank 1957. Never flown. Ultimate fate not known, assumed scrapped at Hatfield.

06037, XK715, Comet C.Mk 2

Built for BOAC and nominated to become Comet 2R (not taken up) 17/03/55. Sold to Ministry of Supply 18/03/55. FF as C.Mk 2 **XK715** 26/04/57. D'd to No.216 Sqn RAF Lyneham 22/05/57 as *Columba*. Loaned to No.51 Sqn 01/05/62 returned to No.216 Sqn 17/09/62. Wfs 29/04/66. Transferred to RAF Cosford for apprentice training as **7905M** 29/04/66. Scrapped West Bromwich, W Midlands May 1973.

06038, Comet 2, Not completed

Built at Hatfield. Laid down for BOAC. Reported to have been moved to Chester.

06039, Comet 2, Not completed

Built at Hatfield. Laid down for LAV of Venezuela 1954. Allocated for RAF fleet reserve 1955. Cocooned. Unclear whether aircraft was completed.

06040, Comet 2, Not completed

Built at Hatfield. Laid down for LAV of Venezuela 1954. Allocated for RAF fleet reserve 1955. Cocooned. Unclear whether aircraft was completed.

06041, Comet 2, Not completed

Built at Hatfield. Laid down for PanAir do Brasil.

06042, Comet 2, Not completed

Built at Hatfield. Laid down for Japan Air Lines.

06043, Comet 2, Not completed

Built at Hatfield. Laid down for Japan Air Lines.

06044, Comet 2, Not completed

Built at Hatfield. Laid down for Japan Air Lines.

06045, XK716, Comet 2/C.Mk 2

First Comet built at Chester. Laid down for UAT, NTU. Sold to Ministry of Supply 18/03/55. FF

as C.Mk 2 **XK716** 06/05/57. D'd to No.216 Sqn RAF Lyneham as *Cepheus* 07/05/57. Wfs April 1967. Flown to RAF Halton for instructional use (re-serialled **7958M**), last flight 04/05/67. Dumped 1972. Scrapped May 1973.

06046, Comet 2

Built at Chester. Fuselage pressure tested 14/03/54. Stored partially finished, then scrapped and used for spares.

06047, Comet 2

Built at Chester. Allocated for RAF fleet reserve 1955. Cocooned, not clear if completed.

06048, Comet 2

Built at Chester. Stored partially completed, used for spares then scrapped 1959.

06049, Comet 2

Built at Chester. Stored partially completed, used for spares then scrapped 1959.

06050 - 06060 Comet 2

Abandoned

06061, Comet 2

Built at Belfast. Laid down for UAT, NTU 1954. Stored at Belfast 1954. Moved to Chester Oct - Nov 1955. Presumed scrapped at Chester.

06062, Comet 2

Built at Belfast. Laid down for UAT, NTU 1954. Stored at Belfast 1954.

Moved to Chester Oct - Nov 1955. Presumed scrapped at Chester.

06063, F-BHAA, Comet 2

Laid down for Air France at Chester, NTU

06064, F-BHAB, Comet 2

Laid down for Air France at Chester, NTU

06065, F-BHAC, Comet 2

Laid down for Air France at Chester, NTU

06066, F-BHAD, Comet 2

Laid down for Air France at Chester, NTU

06067, F-BHAE, Comet 2

Laid down for Air France at Chester, NTU

06068, F-BHAF, Comet 2

Laid down for Air France at Chester, NTU

06069-06070, Comet 2

Not started, due to be built at Chester.

COMET 3

06100, G-ANLO/XP915, Comet 3

Ordered by Ministry of Supply as prototype Comet, **G-ANLO**, FF 19/07/54. World tour in BOAC colours Dec 1955. Re-engined with Avon RA29 13/02/57. FF as modified Comet 3B in BEA colours, named *RMA William Brooks* 21/08/58. Transferred to Air Ministry as **XP915** 25/01/61. To RAE Bedford for BLEU 20/06/61. Wfu 29/03/72, and last flight 04/04/72 with Comet 2E XN453 and Comet 4 XV814. Subsequently used for foam runway arrester trials. Dismantled 04/73. Fuselage moved to BAE Woodford for use as MR.Mk 2 and later AEW.Mk 3 mock up, wings to Halton for apprentice training. Centre section to St Mawgan for BDRT.

06101, Comet 3

First production Comet 3 for BOAC. Not completed. Fuselage used as mock up for interior testing.

06102-06110 Comet 3

Not completed.

COMET 4, 4B, and 4C

06401, G-APDA/9M-AOA/9V-BAS, Comet 4

Hatfield-built. FF 27/04/58, as **G-APDA**. D'd to BOAC 24/02/59. Lsd Ghana Airways *Osagyefo* March 1961. Lsd Middle East Airlines 1962. Purchased Malaysian Airways 09/12/65 and reg'd **9M-AOA**. Re-reg'd **9V-BAS** by Malaysia-Singapore Airlines 07/02/66. Wfu November 1969. Flown to Gatwick 16/11/69 and to Lasham the next day. Sold to Dan-Air Services Ltd 19/11/69. Not flown by Dan-Air and scrapped September 1972.

06402 Comet 4

Built at Hatfield for de Havilland, 1957, never flown. Test airframe for water tank testing 1958. Moved to Hawker-Siddeley for Nimrod mock-up work at Woodford 26/10/64. Moved to dump following trials. Moved to Warton for use as British Aerospace Nimrod 2000 (later MRA.Mk 4) hydraulic test rig, 01/03/97. Scrapped in 2010.

06403, G-APDB/9M-AOB, Comet 4

Hatfield-built. FF 27/07/58 as **G-APDB**. D'd to BOAC 30/09/58. First Eastbound Transatlantic jet service with fare-paying passengers 4/10/58. Sold to Malaysian Airways 11/05/65. Reg'n cx 09/09/65. Re-reg'd **9M-AOB** 10/09/65. Transferred Malaysia-Singapore Airlines 30/12/66. Sold to Dan-Air Services Ltd 15/10/69. Re-reg'd **G-APDB** 17/06/70. Wfs 23/11/73. Donated to Imperial War Museum and flown to Duxford 12/02/74, having flown 36,269 hours, and having made 15,733 landings. The first aircraft in what became the British Airliner Collection. Restored and repainted in BOAC markings 2007. **Aircraft still extant at Duxford in 2022.**

06404, G-APDC/9M-AOC/9V-BAT, Comet 4

Hatfield-built. FF 23/09/58 as **G-APDC**. D'd to BOAC 30/09/58. First Westbound Transatlantic jet service with fare-paying passengers 04/10/58. Chartered Qantas 1962. Lsd Malaysian Airways 1962. Re-reg'd **9M-AOC** 13/10/65. Sold to Malaysian Airways 14/10/65. Re-reg'd **9V-BAT** 22/06/66. Transferred Malaysia-Singapore Airlines 30/12/66. Purchased Dan-Air Services Ltd 29/08/69. Re-reg'd **G-APDC** 18/09/70. Last flight to Lasham 10/04/73. Was to have been social club at Lasham, but scrapped April 1975.

06405, G-APDD/9M-AOD/5Y-AMT, Comet 4

Hatfield-built. FF 05/11/58 as **G-APDD**. D'd to BOAC 18/11/58. Lsd Air Ceylon. Re-reg'd **9M-AOD** 05/11/65. Sold to Malaysian Airways 08/11/65. Transferred Malaysia-Singapore Airlines 30/12/66. D'd to Dan-Air Services Ltd at Gatwick 01/10/69. Re-reg'd **G-APDD** 16/10/69. Lsd East African Airways and re-reg'd **5Y-AMT** 28/12/70. Wfs 22/02/71. Returned to Dan-Air Services Ltd and re-reg'd **G-APDD** 12/03/71. Last flight to Lasham 24/08/72. Scrapped Lasham March 1973.

06406, G-APDE/9M-AOE/9V-BAU/5Y-ALF, Comet 4

First Chester-built Comet 4. FF 20/09/58 as **G-APDE**. D'd to BOAC 02/10/58. Re-reg'd

9M-AOE 29/09/65. Sold to Malaysian Airways 05/10/65. Re-reg'd **9V-BAU** 02/03/66. Transferred Malaysia-Singapore Airlines 30/12/66. Sold to Dan-Air Services Ltd 19/11/69. Lsd East African Airways 22/02/70 and re-reg'd **5Y-ALF**. Returned to Dan-Air Services Ltd (training unit) November 1970 and reg'n **G-APDE** restored 03/03/71. Wfs 02/04/72. Scrapped Lasham April 1973.

06407, G-APDF/XV814, Comet 4

Hatfield-built. FF as **G-APDF** 11/12/58. D'd to BOAC 31/12/58. Lsd Air Ceylon. Lsd Malaysian Airways 1965. Sold to Royal Aircraft Establishment January 1967. Transferred to military marks **XV814** 01/03/67. Delivered Farnborough 07/10/68, modified for radio trials. Entered service with RAE 02/02/71. Used to test RAE SLIS (Sideways Looking Intercept System). Underbelly pod affected stability, and so a Nimrod type fin was installed at Chester from Jun-Oct 71. Wingtip pitot static system fitted Jan-March 1972. Painted in 'raspberry ripple' scheme 1976. Used for testing Nimrod sortie profiles 1981. 1986-87 gained fin-top pod (from XV147). Wfu Farnborough 18/12/92. Last flight from Farnborough to Boscombe Down 28/01/93. Stripped for spares to support last flying Comet, XS235. Sold to Milver Metals 01/07/97. Broken up at Boscombe Down 12/08/97. Many parts to Museum of Flight in Seattle. Nose sold to private collector Chipping Camden 13/08/97. Tail and rear fuselage sold to British Aerospace Warton 03/09/97. Tail dumped Warton early 1999. Tail scrapped 19/09/00. **Nose extant with private owner in Chipping Camden in 2022.**

06408, LV-PLM/LV-AHN, Comet 4

Hatfield-built and originally reg'd G-APDG (NTU) 01/10/57, re-reg'd provisionally **LV-PLM** for Aerolineas Argentinas. FF 27/01/59. D'd Aerolineas Argentinas *Las Tres Marias* 02/03/59 and re-reg'd **LV-AHN**. Wfs 18/09/70. Sold to Dan-Air Services Ltd for spares 04/12/71. Last flight to Lasham 09/12/71. Scrapped January 1973.

06409, G-APDH, Comet 4

Chester-built Comet 4. G-APDF 02/05/57 NTU. Reallocated to BOAC as **G-APDH** 01/10/57. FF 21/11/58. D'd to BOAC 06/12/58. Lsd Qantas. Lsd Malaysian Airways 1964. W/o after crash landing at Changi 22/03/64. Scrapped 1964.

06410, LV-PLO/LV-AHO, Comet 4

Hatfield built. G-APDI 01/10/57 NTU. Provisionally re-reg'd **LV-PLO** for Aerolineas Argentinas. FF 25/02/59. D'd Aerolineas Argentinas *Lucero de la Tarde* 18/03/59. Re-reg'd **LV-AHO** March 1959 and renamed *Cruz del Sur*. W/o Ezeiza Airport, Buenos Aires 20/02/60, after heavy landing and landing gear collapse.

06411, LV-PLP/LV-AHP, Comet 4

Hatfield built. G-APDJ 01/10/57 NTU. Provisionally re-reg'd **LV-PLP** for Aerolineas Argentinas. FF 24/03/59. D'd Aerolineas Argentinas *Elcucero del Alba* 02/05/59. Re-reg'd **LV-AHP**. Accident Paraguay 27/08/59. Salvage declared not commercially viable due to extensive damage.

06412, G-APDK/5Y-ALD, Comet 4

Chester-built. G-APDG 02/05/57 NTU. Reallocated to BOAC as **G-APDK** 01/10/57. FF 01/02/59. D'd to BOAC 12/02/59. Lsd Middle East Airlines 01/11/60. Returned to BOAC 31/03/61. Lsd Air Ceylon 1963. Sold to Dan-Air Services Ltd 19/05/66. Lsd East African Airways 09/01/70 and re-reg'd **5Y-ALD**.

Returned Dan-Air Services Ltd 21/03/70. Re-reg'd **G-APDK** 24/09/70. Wfs 07/05/73. Donated Air Scouts Lasham March 1974. Scrapped September 1980.

06413, G-APDL/5Y-ADD, Comet 4

Hatfield-built. G-APDH 02/05/57 NTU. Reallocated to BOAC as **G-APDL** 01/10/57. FF 27/04/59. D'd to BOAC 06/05/59. Chartered Qantas 1960. Chartered Middle East Airlines. Lsd East African Airways 08/10/65 and re-reg'd **5Y-ADD**. Sold to Dan-Air Services Ltd 14/01/69. W/o in landing accident at Newcastle Airport (landed gear up) 07/10/70. Scrapped Newcastle 1971.

06414, G-APDM/OD-AEV/9V-BBJ, Comet 4

Chester-built. G-APDI 02/05/57 NTU. Reallocated to BOAC as **G-APDM** 01/10/57. FF 21/03/59. D'd to BOAC 16/04/59. Chartered Qantas 1960. Lsd Air Ceylon. Lsd Malaysian Airways 1965. Last BOAC Comet flight (NZ-London) 22/11/65 and wfs 24/11/65. Leased MEA 24/03/67 and re-reg'd **OD-AEV**. Leased Malaysia-Singapore Airlines 20/01/68 and re-reg'd **9V-BBJ**. Re-reg'd **G-APDM**. Sold to Dan-Air Services Ltd 07/01/69. Wfs 08/10/73. Scrapped Gatwick, nose retained February 1984. Nose to NEAM Sunderland July 1984. Nose scrapped on site July 1985 on promise of a larger nose section that did not materialise.

06415, G-APDN, Comet 4

Hatfield-built. G-APDJ 02/05/57 NTU. Reallocated to BOAC as **G-APDN** 01/10/57. FF 29/05/59. Lsd Air Ceylon. Lsd Malaysian Airways. Lsd Kuwait Airways November 1965. Restored BOAC February 1966. Sold to Dan-Air Services Ltd October 1967. Crashed near Barcelona killing all seven crew and 105 passengers 03/07/70.

06416, G-APDO, Comet 4

Chester-built. G-APDK 02/05/57 NTU. Reallocated to BOAC as **G-APDO**. FF 29/04/59. D'd to BOAC 14/05/59. Chartered Air India 1962 - 1963. Wfs 25/09/65. Lease-purchased by Dan-Air Services Ltd 26/05/66. Wfs 26/06/73. Scrapped Lasham June 1974.

06417, G-APDP/9V-BBH/XX944, Comet 4

Chester-built. FF 29/05/59 as **G-APDP**. D'd to BOAC 11/06/59. Lsd Qantas 1959. Lsd Air Ceylon 1962. Lsd Malaysian Airways 1965 and re-reg'd **9V-BBH**. Restored to **G-APDP** BOAC 23/01/68. Dan-Air Services Ltd lease-purchased 13/02/69. Wfs 22/03/73. Transferred to military 08/06/73. D'd RAE Farnborough 19/07/73 and serial **XX944** given. Allocated A&AEE Boscombe Down 26/09/73 and delivered 5/10/73. Allocated to RAE 02/04/74 but remained at A&AEE on charge to RAE. Returned to RAE Farnborough 24/07/74. Wfu 25/04/75 after extensive corrosion/fatigue discovered. RAE apprentice training May 1977. Noted carrying both reg'n G-APDP and serial XX944 1982. Scrapped 09/08/84.

06418, G-APDR/XA-NAZ/XA-NAP, Comet 4

Chester-built. G-APDL 02/05/57 NTU. Reallocated to BOAC as **G-APDR** 14/10/57. FF 09/07/59. D'd to BOAC 20/07/59. Lsd Qantas 1960. Lsd Malayan Airways 1962. Chartered Malaysian Airways 1963. Sold to Mexicana Airways 03/12/64 and re-reg'd **XA-NAZ**. Re-reg'd **XA-NAP** by 1966. Sold to Channel Airways for spares 25/06/71. British Airports Authority Fire School June 1972. Main fire airframe at Stansted 1970s. Scrapped/burnt 1981.

06419, G-APDS/XW626, Comet 4

Chester-built. FF 06/08/59. D'd to BOAC 14/08/59. Lsd Malaysian Airways 1965. Lsd Air Ceylon

late 1965. Lsd Kuwait Airways November 1965. Restored BOAC February 1966. Lsd Middle East Airlines 1966-67. Sold to MoD (Boscombe Down for radar trials) 27/01/69. Transferred to military marks as **XW626** 24/02/69. FF after modifications (including Nimrod type fin and provision for a ventral equipment pannier) 16/06/72. D'd Boscombe Down July 1972. D'd Hawker Siddeley Woodford for AEW mods 02/04/76. FF with AEW nose 28/06/77. SBAC show 1978. RSRE Pershore 1979. RAE Bedford 26/05/80. Last flight 29/08/81. Scrapped at Bedford 11/04/94 after 14 years in open storage.

06420, G-APDT/XA-POW/XA-NAB, Comet 4

Chester-built. G-APDM 02/05/57 NTU. Reallocated to BOAC as **G-APDT** 14/10/57. FF 02/10/59. D'd to BOAC 19/10/59. Lsd Qantas. Lsd Air Ceylon. Lsd Malaysian Airways. Lsd Mexicana 25/11/65 and re-reg'd **XA-POW**, later **XA-NAB**. Returned BOAC 06/12/69. Repainted as G-APDT but not formally registered. Allocated to BOAC Apprentice Training London Heathrow then British Airways Apprentice Training September 1972. British Airports Authority Fire Dept. April 1980. Scrapped London Heathrow 30/08/90.

06421, G-APMA, Comet 4B

Hatfield-built. FF 27/06/59. Loaned to BEA for London-Paris Bleriot Anniversary Air Race, which it subsequently won 19/07/59. D'd to BEA *Sir Edmund Halley* 23/12/59. After testing, it started first London-Nice jet service on 01/04/60. First scheduled service to Oslo and Stockholm 01/07/60. One of final two BEA Comet 4Bs (with G-APME). Last BEA Comet flight from Malaga to LHR on 31/10/71. Scrapped London Heathrow 18/07/72. Bulk of Aircraft to Coley's scrapyard. Nose to BA apprentice school Cranebank, scrapped 1987.

06422, G-APMB, Comet 4B

Hatfield-built. FF 17/08/59. D'd to BEA *Walter Gale* 09/11/59. Lsd Olympic Airways 1964. Wfu Cambridge 05/03/69. Sold to Channel Airways 25/06/70. Wfs 17/01/72. Sold to Dan-Air Services Ltd 09/04/72. Wfs (remained at Gatwick) 28/12/78. Sold to Gatwick Handling 28/12/78. Gatwick Handling absorbed by Aviance UK. Scrapped in July 2004.

06423, G-APMC, Comet 4B

Hatfield-built. FF 01/10/59. Handed over ceremonially at LHR 16/10/59, then formally d'd to BEA as *Andrew Crommelin* 16/11/59. To Marshall 15/07/69 for repaint in BEA Airtours colours, returning 25/09/69. D'd to BEA Airtours January 1970. Sold to Dan-Air Services Ltd 01/11/73. Did not enter service and scrapped at Lasham April 1974.

06424, G-AOVU/XA-NAR/N888WA, Comet 4C

Hatfield-built. G-APDN 02/05/57 NTU. Scheduled to become Comet 4B G-APMD for BEA, but NTU 15/04/58, and instead completed as first Comet 4C. FF reg'd as **G-AOVU** to de Havilland Aircraft Co Ltd 31/10/59. Re-reg'd **XA-NAR**. D'd to Mexicana 08/06/60. Inaugural Golden Aztec service from Mexico City to LAX 04/07/60. Lsd Guest Aerovias SA. Wfs 01/12/70. Property of Boeing (traded for Boeing 727) 1972. Re-reg'd **N888WA** and sold to WesternAir, Albuquerque 17/07/73. Sold to Redmond Air 1978. Wfu Paine Field, Everett July 1979. Donated Everett Community College 1984. Painted in BOAC colours with EVCC in place of registration. Donated Museum of Flight Seattle 1995. **Aircraft still extant at Seattle in 2022.**

06425, GAOVV/XA-NAS/N999WA, Comet 4C
Hatfield-built. Scheduled to become Comet 4B G-APME for BEA, but NTU 15/04/58. Re-reg'd de Havilland Aircraft Co Ltd (as Comet 4C) as **G-AOVV**. FF 03/12/59. Re-reg'd **XA-NAS**. D'd Mexicana 14/01/60. Wfu 01/12/70. Property of Boeing (traded for Boeing 727) 1972. Sold to WesternAir 17/07/73. Re-reg'd **N999WA** and sold to Onyx Aviation 30/12/76. Sold to Redmond Air 1976. Sold to Dick Drost 16/12/76. D'd Chicago O'Hare 11/12/76. Scrapped Chicago O'Hare Airport Spring 1993.

06426, G-APMF, Comet 4B
Hatfield-built. G-APDO 02/05/57 NTU. FF **G-APMF** 05/01/60. D'd to BEA *William Finlay* 27/01/60. Lsd Olympic Airways 1966. D'd to BEA Airtours Ltd 01/04/70. Wfs 31/01/73. Sold to Dan-Air Services Ltd 31/01/73. D'd Lasham 31/01/73 and put into service. Wfs and flown to Lasham 05/11/74. Scrapped Lasham 1976.

06427, G-APDG/9K-ACI, Comet 4
Chester-built. FF 20/11/59. D'd to BOAC 28/11/59. Lsd Middle East Airlines 01/11/60. Wfs BOAC London Airport 23/11/65. Re-reg'd **9K-ACI**, sold to Kuwait Airways 22/07/66. Lsd Middle East Airlines 29/12/68. Restored Kuwait Airways 23/05/69. Wfs 29/09/69. Sold to Dan-Air Services Ltd 19/09/70. Wfs Gatwick 29/04/73. Scrapped Lasham June 1974.

06428, G-APDI, Comet 4
Chester-built. FF 07/12/59. D'd to BOAC 18/12/59. Lsd Middle East Airlines. Lsd AREA Ecuador 13/03/66. Wfs Miami International 28/03/68. Sold Shelton Surplus Inc 1970. Sold Commercial Aviation Co. Inc. 1970. Wfu 1970. Scrapped Miami International Airport February 1978.

06429, G-APDJ, Comet 4
Chester-built. FF 23/12/59. D'd to BOAC 11/01/60. Lsd Air Ceylon. Lsd Malaysian Airways 1964. Provisionally allocated to AREA Ecuador, but instead lease-purchased Dan-Air Services Ltd 14/04/67. Wfs 28/11/72. Scrapped Lasham June 1974.

06430, LV-POY/LV-AHR, Comet 4
Hatfield-built. FF 15/02/60. D'd Aerolineas Argentinas *Alborada* 08/03/60, (temporary reg'n **LV-POY**). Re-reg'd **LV-AHR** and renamed *Arco Iris*. Crashed after hitting trees at Sao Paulo Airport and w/o 23/11/61. Twelve crew and 40 passengers killed.

06431, VP-KPJ/5X-AAO, Comet 4
Chester-built. FF 14/07/60. D'd East African Airways as **VP-KPJ** 25/07/60. First EAA London-Nairobi jet service 17/09/60. Re-reg'd **5X-AAO** (Uganda) 04/64. Sold to Dan-Air Services Ltd 16/11/70. Wfu November 1970. Scrapped Lasham February 1973.

06432, LV-POZ/LV-AHS, Comet 4
Chester-built. FF 18/02/60. Aerolíneas Argentinas provisional reg'n **LV-POZ**. Re-reg'd **LV-AHS** and named *Las Tres Marias* March 1960. D'd 19/03/60. Renamed *Alborada* March 1960. Sold to Dan-Air Services Ltd 23/11/71. Reg'd G-AZLW (never carried) 10/01/72. Destroyed by fire Lasham March 1973.

06433, VP-KPK/5H-AAF, Comet 4
Chester-built. FF 28/07/60. D'd East African Airways as **VP-KPK** 06/09/60. Re-reg'd **5H-AAF** (Tanzania) April 1964. Wfs November 1969. Sold to Dan-Air Services Ltd January 1971. Wfu 11/01/71. Scrapped Lasham February 1973.

06434, LV-PPA/LV-AHU/G-AZIY, Comet 4
Chester-built. FF 02/07/60. Aerolíneas Argentinas provisional reg'n **LV-PPA**. Re-reg'd **LV-AHU** and named *Centaurus* July 1960. D'd 26/07/60. Wfs September 1970. Sold to Dan-Air 08/11/1971 and reg'd **G-AZIY**. Wfs 25/11/73. Scrapped Lasham March 1977.

06435, G-APMD, Comet 4B
Hatfield-built. FF 17/03/60, became BEA's second jetliner inaugurating Istanbul service on 01/01/60. Formally d'd to BEA as *William Denning* 29/03/60. D'd to BEA Airtours Ltd 31/03/70. Sold to Dan-Air Services Ltd 12/09/72. Wfs 31/03/75. Scrapped Lasham November 1976.

06436, G-APME, Comet 4B
Hatfield-built. FF 26/04/60. D'd to BEA *John Tebbutt* 10/05/60. Chartered TAP 1960. Lsd Olympic 1966. Lsd BEA Air Tours Ltd 07/08/70. Sold to Dan-Air Services Ltd 24/02/72. First passenger service with Dan-Air 27/04/72. Wfs Manchester 03/04/78. Scrapped Lasham June 1979.

06437, G-APYC/SX-DAK, Comet 4B
Hatfield-built. FF 07/04/60 as **G-APYC**. D'd Olympic Airways *Queen Frederica* 30/04/60 and re-reg'd **SX-DAK**. Wfs Athens 03/69. D'd Cambridge 24/03/69. Sold to BEA 14/08/69 and reg'n **G-APYC** restored. Sold to Channel Airways 26/01/70. Wfs 18/02/72. Sold to Dan-Air Services Ltd 06/04/72. Wfs 27/11/78. Sold to MoD (Army) and used for SAS training at RAF Kemble from 04/12/78. Scrapped by Bird Group at RAF Kemble 17/11/82.

06438, G-APYD/SX-DAL, Comet 4B
Hatfield-built. FF 03/05/60 as **G-APYD**. Re-reg'd **SX-DAL** 03/05/60. D'd Olympic Airways *Queen Olga* 14/05/60. Wfs Athens 03/69. D'd Cambridge 01/04/69. Sold to BEA 01/09/69, reg'n **G-APYD** restored. Sold to Channel Airways Ltd 26/01/70. Sold to Dan-Air Services Ltd 14/04/72. Wfs (after last Comet 4B passenger service) 23/10/79. Sold to Science Museum Wroughton for £10,000, 31/10/79. **Aircraft still extant at Wroughton in 2022.**

06439, SU-ALC, Comet 4C
Chester-built. FF as **SU-ALC** 21/05/60. First Comet d'd to MisrAir 10/06/60. UAA (name change) 23/12/60. Struck ground near Tripoli when attempting to land in below minimum visibility, killing all eight crew and 16 passengers. Aircraft completely destroyed. W/o 02/01/71.

06440, G-APZM/SX-DAN, Comet 4B
Hatfield-built. G-APMG 15/04/58 NTU. Reallocated BEA **G-APZM**, FF 30.06/60. Lsd Olympic Airways 14/07/60. Re-reg'd **SX-DAN** 06/06/66. Wfs Athens 03/69. D'd Cambridge for storage 27/03/69. Returned BEA 10/10/69, reg'n **G-APZM** restored. Sold to Channel Airways 14/05/70. Sold to Dan-Air Services Ltd 17/04/72. Wfs Gatwick 12/11/78. Scrapped Lasham September 1980.

06441, SU-ALD, Comet 4C
Chester-built. FF 15/06/60. D'd MisrAir 29/06/60. UAA (name change) 23/12/60. Pilot lost control in severe turbulence and crashed into sea 15km from Bombay, 28/07/63. 8 crew and 55 passengers killed.

06442, G-APMG, Comet 4B
Hatfield-built. FF 25/07/60. D'd to BEA *John Grigg* 31/07/60. Lsd Olympic Airways 1960s various. D'd to BEA Air Tours Ltd 16/03/70. Lsd BEA, returned BEA Air Tours Ltd 1973. Sold to Dan-Air Services Ltd 19/01/73. Wfs 16/11/77. Scrapped Lasham 15/04/78.

06443, G-ARBB/XA-NAT/N777WA, Comet 4C
Hatfield-built. Reg'd **G-ARBB** 27/04/60. FF 07/10/60. Re-reg'd **XA-NAT** and d'd to Mexicana 29/11/60. Lsd Guest Aerovias Mexico SA 1961. Wfu 01/12/70 after undercarriage collapse on landing. Sold to WesternAir April 1973 and re-reg'd **N777WA**. Transferred to Distribute Air 1977. Sold to Redmond Air November 1979. Derelict Mexico City 1994. To Parque Hidalgo Zoo at Irapuato, north of Mexico City, as children's playground.

06444, SU-ALE, Comet 4C
Chester-built. FF 22/11/60. D'd to United Arab Airlines 23/12/60. Crashed on take-off from Munich 09/02/70, no fatalities. Scrapped on airfield 26/05/70.

06445, OD-ADR, Comet 4C
Hatfield-built. OD-ADK NTU. Re-reg'd **OD-ADR** before completion 1960. FF 03/12/60. D'd to Middle East Airlines 19/12/60. Destroyed during Israeli commando attack on Beirut Airport 28/12/68.

06446, OD-ADQ, Comet 4C
Chester-built. G-ARJH NTU. FF 04/02/61 as **OD-ADQ**. D'd to Middle East Airlines 15/02/61. Destroyed during Israeli attack 28/12/68.

06447, G-ARDI/SX-DAO, Comet 4C
Hatfield-built. FF 18/03/61. D'd to BEA 25/03/61. Lsd Olympic Airways *Princess Sophia* 25/03/63 and re-reg'd **SX-DAO**. Wfs Athens 03/69. D'd Cambridge 02/04/69. Re-reg'd **G-ARDI** 16/04/70 and sold to Channel Airways Ltd 17/04/70. Wfs 03/10/71. Sold to Dan-Air Services Ltd April 1972. Scrapped Southend June 1972.

06448, OD-ADS, Comet 4C
Chester-built. FF 05/03/61. D'd to Middle East Airlines 14/03/61. Lsd Kuwait Airways and returned. Destroyed during Israeli attack 28/12/68.

06449, G-ARCO, Comet 4C
Hatfield-built. FF 05/04/61 as **G-ARCO**. D'd to BEA 13/04/61. Destroyed by terrorist bomb off Cyprus on 12/10/67, killing the seven crew and 59 passengers.

06450, OD-ADT, Comet 4B
Chester-built. FF 09/03/61. D'd to Middle East Airlines 18/03/61. Wfs 03/03/73 but used for some charter work until sold to Dan-Air Services Ltd for spares 02/10/73 and flown to Lasham 04/10/73. Scrapped at Lasham June 1974.

06451, G-ARCP/G-BBUV, Comet 4B
Hatfield-built. FF 12/04/61. D'd to BEA *William Brooks* 19/04/61. D'd to BEA Airtours Ltd 22/05/70. Sold to Dan-Air Services Ltd 22/10/73 and re-reg'd **G-BBUV** to avoid confusion with BAC One Eleven G-AXCP, 19/12/73. Wfs Gatwick 22/10/78. Scrapped Lasham October 1979.

06452, G-ARJK, Comet 4B
Chester-built. FF 04/05/61. D'd to BEA 15/05/61. Lsd Olympic Airways. Wfs Autumn 1969. D'd to BEA Airtours Ltd 05/03 /70. Sold to Dan-Air Services Ltd 01/10/73. Wfs Gatwick 01/11/76. Scrapped Lasham October 1977.

06453, G-ARGM, Comet 4B
Hatfield-built. G-AREI 1960 NTU. Reg'd **G-ARGM** 31/08/60. FF 27/04/61. D'd to BEA 06/05/61. Lsd Olympic Airways. D'd to BEA Airtours Ltd 31/03/70. Sold to Dan-Air Services Ltd 01/11/73. Scrapped Lasham April 1975.

06454, SU-ALL, Comet 4C
Chester-built. FF 30/05/61. D'd to United Arab Airlines 12/06/61. Transferred (name change) Egypt Airlines 02/01/71. Wfs Cairo 02/06/75. Sold to Dan-Air Services Ltd October 1976. Dumped Cairo 1976-1977. Removed from Airport and scrapped late 1980s.

06455, G-ARJL, Comet 4B
Hatfield-built. FF 19/05/61. D'd to BEA 31/05/61. Lsd Olympic Airways February 1964. Returned BEA February 1970. Transferred BEA Airtours Ltd 01/03/70. Wfs 31/10/73. Sold to Dan-Air Services Ltd 08/11/73. Scrapped Lasham September 1974.

06456, G-ARJM, Comet 4B
Chester-built. G-ARJE NTU. Reg'd **G-ARJM** 13/02/61. FF 08/06/61. D'd to BEA 26/06/61. Lsd Olympic Airlines 1961. Crashed after stalling on take-off from Ankara-Esenboga Airport 21/12/61. Seven crew and 20 passengers killed; seven passengers survived. (Various parts of damaged aircraft shipped to RAE Farnborough January 1962.)

06457, ST-AAW/G-ASDZ, Comet 4C
Hatfield-built. XA-NAD NTU Mexicana. FF **G-ASDZ** 05/11/62. Re-reg'd **ST-AAW** and d'd to Sudan Airways 11/01/63. Wfs 11/11/72. Sold to Dan-Air Services Ltd 02/06/75 and re-reg'd **G-ASDZ**. Scrapped Lasham October 1976.

06458, SU-ALM/G-BEEX, Comet 4C
Chester-built. FF 30/06/61. D'd to United Arab Airlines 15/07/61. Transferred EgyptAir (name change) 10/10/71. Wfu 30/03/76. Re-reg'd **G-BEEX** 10/09/76 and sold to Dan Air Serviced Ltd 14/10/76. Wfu 15/10/76. Nose sent to BAE Woodford 1977. Remainder scrapped Lasham August 1977. Nose donated Lincolnshire Aviation Museum 1982. Sold to North East Aircraft Museum 1989. **Nose extant with NEAM in 2022.**

06459, G-ARJN, Comet 4B
Hatfield-built. G-ARJF NTU. Reg'd **G-ARJN** BEA 13/02/61. FF 21/07/61. D'd to BEA 04/08/61. Lsd Olympic Airways 1968. Re-reg'd and d'd to BEA Airtours Ltd 25/03/70. Lsd BEA. Sold to Dan-Air Services Ltd 10/02/73. Wfs 22/12/77. Scrapped Lasham November 1978.

06460, G-AROV/LV-PTS/LV-AIB, Comet 4C
Chester-built. Reg'd **G-AROV** 11/08/61. FF 21/08/61. Reg'n cx 20/03/62 and delivered Aerolineas Argentinas (provisional reg'n **LV-PTS**) 27/04/62. Re-reg'd **LV-AIB** May 1962. Sold to

Dan-Air Services Ltd 20/10/71. Wfs Gatwick 29/10/77. Scrapped Lasham November 1978.

06461, SA-R-7, Comet 4C
Hatfield-built. FF 29/03/62. D'd to HM the King Saud of Saudi Arabia 15/06/62. Crashed in the Alps, 20/03/63, striking the Punta Bifida peak of the Catena delle Guide at c.2700 m. Nine crew and nine passengers killed.

06462, SU-AMV, Comet 4C
Chester-built. FF 25/03/62. D'd to United Arab Airlines 06/04/62. Transferred (airline name change) EgyptAir 10/10/71. Wfs Cairo 31/05/76. Sold to Dan-Air Services Ltd October 1976. Scrapped Lasham September 1977.

06463, ST-AAX/G-BDIF, Comet 4C
Hatfield-built. XA-NAE Mexicana NTU. FF 08/12/62. Re-reg'd **ST-AAX** and d'd to Sudan Airways 29/09/67. Wfs November 1972. Sold to Dan-Air Services Ltd 02/06/75 and re-reg'd **G-BDIF** 21/08/75. Wfs 05/11/79. Scrapped Lasham 21/10/80. Nose remained with fire dept, then burned and finally scrapped.

06464, SU-AMW, Comet 4C
Chester-built. FF 03/04/62. D'd to United Arab Airlines 16/04/62. Crashed in Thailand 19/07/62, hitting mountain. Eight crew and 18 passengers killed.

06465, 9K-ACA/G-AYWX, Comet 4C
Chester-built. FF 14/12/62. D'd to Kuwait Airways 18/01/63. Lsd Middle East Airways 29/12/68. Restored Kuwait Airways March 1969. Wfs Beirut 30/10/69. Sold to Dan-Air Services Ltd 27/03/71. Re-reg'd **G-AYWX** 22/04/71. Wfs 29/04/78. Last flight 02/05/78. Scrapped Lasham October 1979.

06466, SU-ANC/G-BEEZ, Comet 4C
Chester-built. FF 08/12/62. D'd to United Arab Airlines 23/12/62. Transferred (Airline name change) EgyptAir 10/10/71. Wfs Cairo 16/12/75. Re-reg'd **G-BEEZ** 10/09/76 and sold to Dan-Air Serviced Ltd 16/10/76. Wfu 16/10/76. Scrapped Lasham November 1977.

06467, XR395/G-BDIT, Comet C.Mk 4
Chester-built. FF as **XR395** 15/11/61. D'd to No.216 Sqn, RAF 01/06/62. Wfu and flown to No.60 MU Leconfield 02/07/75. Re-reg'd **G-BDIT** 01/09/75 and sold to Dan-Air Services Ltd 29/08/75. Wfs 13/10/80. D'd to Doug Arnold at Blackbushe for use as restaurant. 12/06/81. Scrapped Blackbushe July 1984.

06468, XR396/G-BDIU, Comet C.Mk 4
Chester-built. FF as **XR396** 28/12/61. D'd to No.216 Sqn, RAF 01/06/62. Wfu and flown to No.60 MU Leconfield, 03/07/75. Sold to Dan-Air Services Ltd 29/08/75, reg'd as **G-BDIU**. Wfs 06/10/80. Sold to British Aerospace Bitteswell 09/07/81. Broken-up Bitteswell July 1981. Reduced to fuselage May 1982. Nose removed, believed transported to Woodford. Fuselage sections to RAF Kinloss February 1986. Sections at Kinloss scrapped 1996.

06469, XR397/G-BDIV, Comet C.Mk 4
Chester-built. FF as **XR397** 17/01/62. D'd to No.216 Sqn, RAF 14/02/62. Wfs RAF Lyneham 17/06/75. Flown to No.60 MU Leconfield,

21/06/75. Sold to Dan-Air Services Ltd 29/08/75 and reg'd **G-BDIV** 01/09/75. Wfs 12/11/79, flown to Lasham for Dan-Air Historical Association 13/11/79. Last Comet scrapped at Lasham 17/07/85.

06470, XR398/G-BDIW, Comet C.Mk 4
Chester-built. FF as **XR398** 13/02/62. D'd to No.216 Sqn, RAF 16/03/62. Last sortie and wfs 21/06/75. Flown to No.60 MU Leconfield, 30/06/75. Sold to Dan-Air Services Ltd 29/08/75 as **G-BDIW**. Flew world's last commercial Comet flight and wfs 09/11/80. Sold to Air Classik Museum and flown to Düsseldorf 07/02/81. Title transferred to Düsseldorf Airport 03/08/85. Sold and moved by road to L&P Junior's Hermeskeil Museum, Germany, February 1988. **Aircraft still extant at Hermeskeil in 2022.**

06471, XR399/G-BDIX, Comet C.Mk 4
Chester-built. FF as **XR399** 20/03/62. D'd to No.216 Sqn, RAF 26/04/62. Wfs RAF Lyneham 25/06/75. Sold to Dan-Air Services Ltd 29/08/75 and reg'd **G-BDIX** 01/09/75. Wfs Gatwick 17/10/80. Sold to Museum of Flight and d'd to East Fortune 30/09/81. (Complete inspection and repaint 1997.) **Aircraft still extant at East Fortune in 2022.**

06472, VP-KRL/5Y-AAA, Comet 4
Chester-built. Last Comet 4 built. FF 12/03/62. D'd East African Airways 10/04/62. Re-reg'd **5Y-AAA** 24/04/64. Wfs Nairobi 25/01/71. Sold to Dan-Air Services Ltd 08/02/71. Scrapped Lasham February 1973.

06473, XS235, Comet 4C
Chester-built. FF 26/09/63. D'd to MoD A&AEE Boscombe Down (named *Canopus*) 02/12/63. Wfu 14/03/97 after last trials flight. Flown to Bruntingthorpe, Leicestershire 30/10/97 (last ever Comet flight). Gifted to British Aviation Heritage Collection February 1998. **Aircraft still extant at Bruntingthorpe in 2022.**

06474, 9K-ACE/ G-AYVS, Comet 4C
Chester-built. FF 17/12/63. D'd to Kuwait Airways 02/02/64. Wfs Beirut 19/01/69. Lsd Middle East Airlines 28/01/69. Restored Kuwait Airways July 1969. Wfs Beirut 02/09/69. Sold to Dan-Air Services Ltd 20/03/71 and re-reg'd **G-AYVS** 08/04/71. Wfs Gatwick 04/01/77. Scrapped Lasham April 1978.

06475, SU-ANI, Comet 4C
Chester-built. Last civil Comet. FF 04/02/64. D'd to United Arab Airlines 26/02/64. Crashed at Addis Ababa, Ethiopia, 14/01/70. Pilot descended below minima and crashed on landing. No fatalities.

06476, G-5-1/XV147, Comet 4C/Nimrod
Chester-built. Remained unsold as Comet 4C. G-5-2 NTU. FF 25/10/65. Flew Chester to Woodford as Comet 4C **G-5-1**, converted to second Nimrod prototype, allocated serial **XV147**. FF as Nimrod prototype 31/07/67. Retained Avon engines.

06477, XV148, Comet 4C/Nimrod
Chester-built. Remained unsold as Comet 4C. Converted to Nimrod, Chester 1965. FF 23/05/67. **Nose extant with private owner in Guildford in 2022.**